Cuba

Cuba

BY DEBORAH KENT

Enchantment of the World™
Second Series

CHILDREN'S PRESS®

An Imprint of Scholastic Inc.

Frontispiece: **Vintage car, Havana**

Consultant: Adrián López-Denis, PhD, Managing Director–Cuba, Nexo Ventures
Please note: All statistics are as up-to-date as possible at the time of publication.

Book production by The Design Lab

Library of Congress Cataloging-in-Publication Data
Kent, Deborah.
 Cuba / by Deborah Kent.
     pages cm. — (Enchantment of the world)
 Includes bibliographical references and index.
 Audience: Grades 4–6.
 ISBN 978-0-531-21694-1 (library binding : alk. paper)
 1. Cuba—Juvenile literature. I. Title.
 F1758.5.K36 2015
 972.91—dc23   2015000526

1 2 3 4 5 6 7 8 9 10 R 25 24 23 22 21 20 19 18 17 16

Musician in Havana

Contents

CHAPTER 1   Fighting for Freedom **8**

CHAPTER 2   The Most Beautiful Country **12**

CHAPTER 3   From Hummingbirds to Crocodiles **24**

CHAPTER 4   Then and Now **36**

CHAPTER 5   The Power of the Party **66**

CHAPTER 6   Waiting in Line **76**

CHAPTER 7   Who Are Los Cubanos? **86**

CHAPTER 8   Prayers and Spirits **94**

CHAPTER 9   Body, Heart, and Mind **102**

CHAPTER 10 Among Compañeros........................... **116**

Timeline...................................... **128**

Fast Facts **130**

To Find Out More............................. **134**

Index **136**

Left to right: **Produce stand, harvesting sugarcane, Labor Day parade, circling the sacred ceiba tree, Isla de la Juventud**

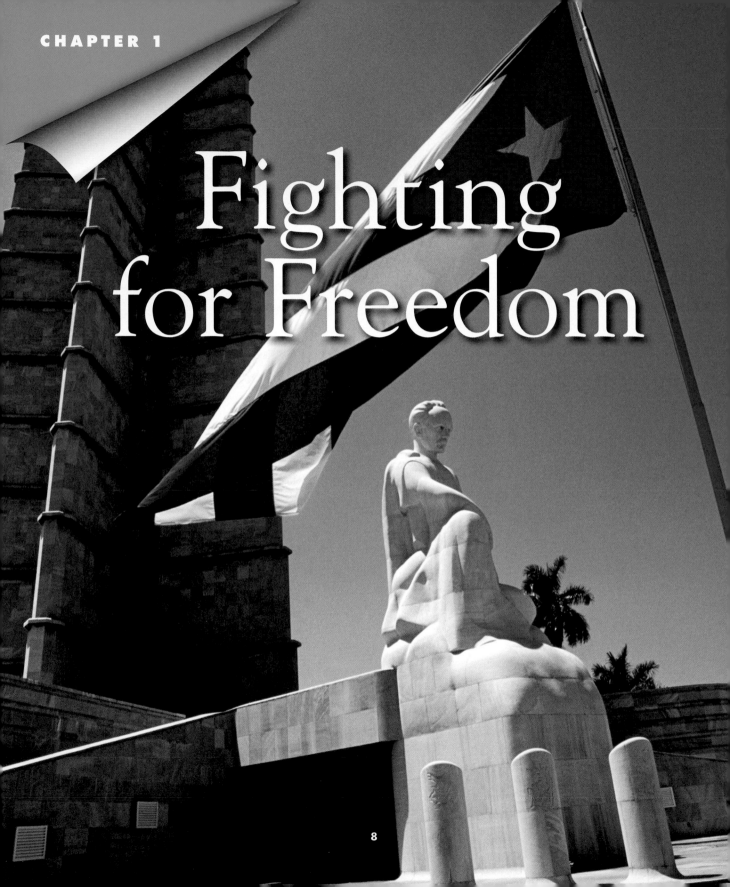

CHAPTER 1

Fighting for Freedom

EACH YEAR ON JANUARY 1, CUBANS CELEBRATE Triumph of the Revolution Day, a day that honors the revolution that transformed Cuban society in 1959. In years past, as many as one million people packed Revolution Square in Havana, the capital of Cuba, to hear a speech by Fidel Castro, who served as Cuba's leader from 1959 until 2008.

Revolution Square is flanked by the National Library on the east and the National Theater on the west. Towering above the square is the José Martí Memorial, a monument to Cuba's most revered national hero.

José Martí was born in Havana in 1853. At the time of his birth, Cuba had been ruled by Spain for more than three hundred years. Like many Cubans, Martí felt that Spain exploited his homeland. He longed to see Cuba become independent. When he was only sixteen he started a newspaper called *La*

Opposite: **The memorial to José Martí, in Havana's Revolution Square, was completed in 1959.**

Patria Libre (The Free Fatherland). For his outspoken views, the Spanish authorities arrested him and threw him into prison.

When Martí was released several months later, he left Cuba for a life in exile. Eventually he settled in the United States, where he wrote about Cuba's plight and worked to organize an uprising against Spain. Finally, in 1895, he returned to Cuba, hoping to spark a revolution. Only three weeks later he was shot and killed by Spanish troops in a skirmish at the town of Dos Ríos.

"Those who have you, o Liberty, do not know you," José Martí once wrote. "Those who do not have you should not speak of you, but win you." Today José Martí is honored throughout Cuba and the world as a revolutionary and a champion of human rights. In Revolution Square, Cubans can gaze at the monument to their national hero and remember the cause of freedom for which he lived and died.

A poet, essayist, and philosopher, José Martí helped organize the movement for Cuban independence.

CHAPTER 2

The Most Beautiful Country

WHEN EXPLORER CHRISTOPHER COLUMBUS set foot on the island of Cuba in 1492, he was astonished by the land that lay before him. In his journal he wrote, "This country is the most beautiful that human eyes have ever seen." Columbus and his men were dazzled by the gleaming white beaches, warm breezes, palm trees, and fields of wildflowers. Today, more than five centuries later, Cuba still amazes visitors with its natural beauty.

Opposite: **The warm waters of the Caribbean Sea lap against the southern coast of Cuba.**

The Lay of the Land

Cuba is the largest island in the Caribbean Sea. It is shaped somewhat like a lizard, with its tail pointing toward Mexico and its head reaching toward the Atlantic Ocean. Slightly smaller than the U.S. state of Pennsylvania, Cuba is 777 miles (1,250 kilometers) in length and 119 miles (192 km) at its widest point. The island lies some 90 miles (145 km) south of Florida, making it one of the closest neighbors of the United States.

What's in a Name?

Scholars debate the origin of the name Cuba. Although no one is sure where it came from or what it means, most historians believe the name was used by the Taíno people who lived on the island when Columbus arrived. The name probably came from a term meaning "great place" or "place of fertile land."

Many tourists visit Isla de la Juventud to relax on its beautiful beaches.

Cuba is part of an island chain called the West Indies. It is the largest island in the group. More than 1,600 smaller islands surround the main island of Cuba. Many of these off-shore islands are merely rocks jutting above the water. The

Cuba's Geographic Features

Area: 42,804 square miles (110,862 sq km)

Length of Coastline: About 2,100 miles (3,400 km)

Greatest Distance East to West: 777 miles (1,250 km)

Greatest Distance North to South: 119 miles (192 km)

Highest Elevation: Turquino Peak, 6,476 feet (1,974 m)

Lowest Elevation: Sea level along the coast

Longest River: Cauto, 230 miles (370 km)

Largest Lake: Leche Lagoon, 26 square miles (67 sq km)

Average Daily High Temperature: In Havana, 78°F (26°C) in January, 88°F (31°C) in July

Average Daily Low Temperature: In Havana, 66°F (19°C) in January, 75°F (24°C) in July

Average Annual Precipitation: 54 inches (137 cm)

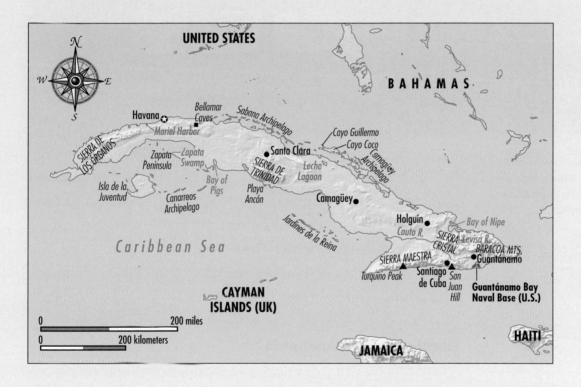

largest offshore island is Isla de la Juventud (the Isle of Youth), which sprawls over about 934 square miles (2,419 sq km) and has about eighty-five thousand inhabitants.

The steep Sierra Maestra rises sharply from Cuba's southern coast.

With its long coastline, Cuba has many fine natural harbors, which are sheltered inlets where ships can anchor and avoid stormy seas. The greatest of the nation's harbors is Havana Harbor, which has served as a port since the 1500s. Other major harbors include Cienfuegos, Matanzas, Manzanillo, and Santiago de Cuba.

Highlands and Lowlands

Three mountain ranges cross the island, dividing it into western, central, and eastern sections. The Sierra de Los Órganos stands in the northwest, the Sierra de Trinidad crosses the center of the island, and the Sierra Maestra rises in the southeast. The nation's highest point, Turquino Peak, reaches 6,476 feet (1,974 meters) in the Sierra Maestra.

Viñales Valley in central-western Cuba features oddly shaped hills called *mogotes*. These steep-sided hills rise suddenly from the flat land around them.

About two-thirds of the island of Cuba is covered by relatively flat plains. Much of these lowlands has been heavily farmed. A unique feature of Cuba's lowlands is the Zapata Swamp, a vast

The mogotes in Viñales Valley formed about 160 million years ago as much of the limestone in the landscape dissolved, leaving behind only a few hills.

Guantánamo

At the eastern tip of Cuba stands the Guantánamo Bay Naval Base. Guantánamo, or "Gitmo" as U.S. personnel call it, is under the control of the United States government. The United States and Cuba signed a treaty to establish a military base at Guantánamo in 1903. The Cuban government is generally opposed to this U.S. presence, and the status of Guantánamo remains a point of hostility between the two countries.

wetland that covers a peninsula on the island's southeastern coast. Most Cubans live in cities in the lowland regions.

River and Sea

More than six hundred rivers and streams flow over the main island of Cuba. Most of them are too shallow for boats to travel on. The longest river, the Cauto River, runs about 230 miles (370 km) in the southeastern part of the island.

Zapata Swamp

Zapata Swamp National Park is in Matanzas Province on the Zapata Peninsula in southern Cuba. Spreading over an area larger than the U.S. state of Rhode Island, it is the largest protected area in Cuba and in all of the Caribbean. Zapata includes beaches, rain forests, rivers, and ponds. It is a refuge for nearly nine hundred plant species and many birds and animals, including the Zapata wren, the Zapata rail, and the Cuban crocodile.

A Natural Wonder

One of Cuba's most spectacular natural wonders is the network of caverns in Matanzas Province, near Varadero Beach, called the Bellamar Caves. In these caverns, rock formations called stalagmites and stalactites create elaborate natural sculptures. The walls of passageways are adorned with sparkling crystal formations. Two natural springs bear romantic names: the Fountain of Youth and the Fountain of Love.

More than three hundred beaches grace Cuba's coastline. Some are lonely, undeveloped stretches of sand and sea that are ideal for hiking or a solitary swim. Others have been developed into resorts that feature restaurants, hotels, and nightclubs. Playa Ancón, or Ancón Beach, is a popular spot near the lively town of Trinidad. Cayo Coco and Cayo Guillermo are islands off the north coast and are reached by driving over a causeway. Their unspoiled beaches are wonderful for snorkeling and scuba diving. Varadero Beach is a resort with a 13-mile (21 km) stretch of sand.

Sun and Storms

Cuba enjoys lavish sunshine and a mild climate. In the summer the average temperature is 80 degrees Fahrenheit (27 degrees Celsius). The average daily temperature in the winter is about 70°F (21°C). However, Cuba can be subject to chilly winter days and nights. Houses have no central heating, so

A Quick Tour of Cuba's Cities

Havana is Cuba's capital and largest city, home to more than 2 million people. Santiago de Cuba, often known simply as Santiago, had an estimated population of 555,865 in 2014, making it Cuba's second-largest city. In the 1500s Santiago was the major Spanish settlement in Cuba. Today, it remains one of Cuba's major ports. Santiago is known for its Afro-Cuban culture, and it is a center for music. San Pedro de la Roca del Morro Castle (below) is one of the best surviving examples of seventeenth-century Spanish architecture. It is an imposing complex of walls, towers, parade grounds, and magazines for storing weapons and gunpowder.

With about 347,562 inhabitants, Camagüey (above) is Cuba's third-largest city. Centuries ago pirates such as the Welshman Henry Morgan raided this Spanish settlement. As a defense against the marauders, villagers laid out their central streets in a confusing, twisting pattern. Today, a visitor can follow these streets and discover hidden plazas, churches, and shops. Camagüey is the largest city in Cuba's interior. It remains an important center of industry and agricultural trade.

Cuba's fourth-largest city, Holguín, has about 319,102 residents. It is called the City of Parks because four major plazas, or city squares, grace the city's center. Holguín is a center of manufacturing in eastern Cuba. Food processing is a major industry in the city, and furniture, ceramics, and cigars are all made there.

such cold snaps are a hardship. When the temperature drops below 50°F (10°C), people sometimes huddle in their homes and light the burners of their stoves for heat.

Rainfall in Cuba is seasonal. The rainy season begins in May and lasts through October. The dry season stretches from November through April. Droughts are common and sometimes spell disaster for farmers. Rainfall is generally heavier in the mountains than it is along the coasts. Yearly rainfall for the island as a whole averages about 54 inches (137 centimeters).

The temperature in Cuba is sometimes chilly enough that people wear sweaters.

Although Cuba has what many people consider an ideal climate, it also can have violent weather. Cuba lies in the path of frequent tropical storms and hurricanes. Hurricanes usually strike the island in August or September. They bring towering waves and destructive winds that can level buildings and destroy crops.

Five major hurricanes struck Cuba in 2008, the stormiest year in modern history. In 2012 Hurricane Sandy swept over Cuba and neighboring islands. Sandy's winds topped 100

A woman shelters herself as she crosses the street in Havana during a September rainstorm. September is one of the rainiest months in Cuba.

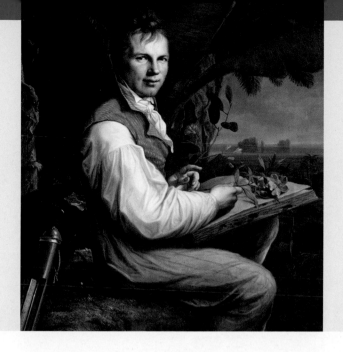

Alexander von Humboldt

Cuba's Alejandro de Humboldt National Park is named in honor of the German naturalist and explorer Friedrich Wilhelm Heinrich Alexander von Humboldt (1769–1859). During an expedition to Latin America, von Humboldt visited Cuba for several months in 1800 and 1801, carefully studying Cuba's landforms, plants, and animals. He also gathered data on Cuba's population, sugar production, and trade. Because of the vast amount of geographic and economic information he collected, he is sometimes called "the second discoverer of Cuba."

miles per hour (160 kilometers per hour) and killed a total of 285 people, 11 of them in Cuba.

Debris litters the streets of Santiago de Cuba, Cuba's second-largest city, after Hurricane Sandy struck in 2012. The storm damaged half the houses in the city.

CHAPTER 3

From Hummingbirds to Crocodiles

EACH YEAR THOUSANDS OF VISITORS COME TO CUBA to enjoy nature. They are drawn by the nation's rich diversity of flora and fauna. Because Cuba is an island, many of its plants and animals evolved in isolation. About three thousand of Cuba's plant species are endemic, meaning that they are found nowhere else in the world. Cuba has sixteen endemic mammals, twenty-three endemic birds, and 124 endemic reptiles and amphibians.

Opposite: **The shimmering green Cuban emerald hummingbird is widespread in Cuba, where it is known as the zunzún.**

The Trees of Cuba

About one-quarter of the land in Cuba is forested. Virtually none of this is primary forest, however. All the forests that covered the island when Europeans first arrived there were cut down over the centuries to plant crops. Beginning in the 1960s, however, Cuba replanted much of the land.

From Hummingbirds to Crocodiles **25**

National Tree

Cuba's national tree is the royal palm, which can reach heights of 90 feet (30 m). It can shoot up as much as 1 foot (30 centimeters) in a single year. The leaves of the royal palm sometimes stretch to lengths of 16 feet (5 m). During the summer months, the royal palm is crowned with spectacular yellow blossoms.

Cuba's rain forest contains many cooling waterfalls, including El Nicho Falls near Cienfuegos, in the south.

Today, pine forests grow in the western part of the island, in Pinar del Río Province. Smaller pine forests are found around the Sierra Cristal and Baracoa Mountains in the east. Pine forests also stand on the Isla de la Juventud. Elsewhere,

moist forests grow. Some of the trees in these forests drop their leaves during the dry months of winter.

One of Cuba's most cherished trees is the ceiba, or kapok. The ceiba can reach a height of 200 to 300 feet (60 to 90 m), and its trunk can be 10 feet (3 m) thick. The seed pods of the ceiba are surrounded with a light, fluffy fiber. This fiber was long used to stuff mattresses, pillows, toys, and life preservers, although in recent times ceiba fiber has been replaced by synthetic materials.

The royal poinciana is not native to Cuba. It originated in Madagascar, a large island off the east coast of Africa. It is often planted in Cuban gardens and along roadsides. Its spreading, leafy branches produce shade that is highly welcome on Cuba's hot summer days.

Cuba's Flowers

In October 2012, botanists announced the discovery of two new orchid species in Cuba. The first, given the scien-

The National Flower

The white ginger lily is Cuba's national flower. In Spanish it is known as the *flor de mariposa* (butterfly flower) because its spreading white petals look like the wings of a butterfly. A native of the mountains of South Asia, the white ginger lily was brought to Cuba as a garden flower. It has gone wild and now flourishes in Cuba's mountainous regions.

tific name *Tetramicra riparia*, grows in the remote forests of Baracoa, at the eastern tip of the island. It has tiny white flowers that are almost hidden among the rocks and foliage. The second new species, called *Encyclia navarroi*, contrasts strikingly with the first species. It has large, purple and green petals and somewhat resembles a daffodil. It grows in forests along Cuba's western coast. Altogether, Cuba has more than three hundred orchid species.

Orchids make up only a small portion of Cuba's wildflowers. Experts estimate that Cuba has nearly eight thousand species of flowering plants.

The showy chalice vine is one of Cuba's many endemic flower species. At night its coconut-like fragrance fills the air. Although this plant is lovely to look at, its leaves and flowers are poisonous.

The yellow morning glory is a common vine found all over Cuba. Its clusters of bell-shaped flowers adorn gardens from December to March.

Claws and Fur

Cuba has few native land mammals. There are no squirrels, rabbits, raccoons, or opossums. Rats and mice are widespread, but they were introduced by Europeans hundreds of years ago.

Hutias, on the other hand, are native to Cuba and other islands in the Caribbean. Hutias are a family of large rodents. The Desmarest's hutia is endemic to Cuba. It has thick, black or brown fur and looks like a large rat with a furry tail. The Desmarest's hutia has been under government protection since 1968, and today it is abundant throughout Cuba. It lives well in captivity and sometimes has been raised for its meat. Other hutias found in Cuba include the Cabrera's hutia, eared hutia, dwarf hutia, and San Felipe hutia.

Bats are another common family of mammals in Cuba. At sundown thousands of bats flutter over Cuba's fields and vil-

Back from the Brink

The Cuban solenodon is one of the rarest mammals in Cuba. Solenodons are among the very few mammals whose bite is poisonous. The solenodon eats insects, worms, and small lizards, which it finds by probing into holes and crevices with its long, flexible nose. It kills its prey with its poisonous saliva. For many years, scientists believed that the Cuban solenodon had gone extinct. Then, in 2003, a healthy specimen was discovered in Cuba's eastern forests. Little is known of the Cuban solenodon's behavior because the animal is so rare and only comes out at night, so is rarely seen.

lages, snatching insects on the wing. Among the more than twenty species found in Cuba are the bulldog bat, pallid bat, big brown bat, eastern red bat, vesper bat, and western mastiff bat.

Several kinds of mammals also live in the waters around Cuba. The endangered West Indian manatee is a huge creature that swims slowly through shallow water, grazing on plants that grow on the seafloor. Several kinds of whales and porpoises swim in Cuba's coastal waters, including the humpback whale, sei whale, and bottlenose dolphin.

Desmarest's hutias live in a wide variety of landscapes ranging from rain forests to coastal swamps to grasslands.

A Good Idea Gone Wrong

The small Indian mongoose is a slender, weasel-like mammal with dark brown fur and a bushy tail. It is native to India, Afghanistan, and other parts of Asia. During the 1800s the mongoose was introduced to Cuba, Puerto Rico, and other islands in the Caribbean. Because the mongoose is a fierce hunter, farmers hoped it would destroy the rats that infested their sugarcane fields and the snakes that attacked their chickens. Instead, it turned out that the mongoose was an expert at killing the chickens it was meant to protect. Furthermore, it preyed on native birds, frogs, and lizards, and on the rare Cuban solenodon, a small shrewlike mammal. The mongoose is highly adaptable, and it reproduces quickly. Though it seemed like a good idea back in the 1800s, introducing the mongoose into nonnative areas has instead proved to be an environmental disaster.

A World of Birds

Cuba is home to more than 130 bird species, ranging from tiny hummingbirds to tall, graceful flamingos. The bee hummingbird, known to Cubans as the *zunzuncito*, is the world's smallest known bird. When fully grown it is not much larger than a bumblebee, extending only 2 inches (5 cm) in length and weighing less than a U.S. dime. The bee hummingbird is endemic to Cuba, living in forests and woodlands on the main island.

The Cuban tody is a small, colorful bird that thrives in many environments, including pine forests, dry lowlands, and coastal rain forests. Todies nest in hollow trees or in tunnels about 1 foot (30 cm) in length that they dig into the banks of streams.

The vivid Cuban tody features many distinct patches of color.

Tragically, many of Cuba's birds are endangered because of the destruction of their natural habitat. These include the giant kingbird and the Cuban solitaire.

In addition to habitat loss, the Cuban Amazon parrot has to contend with poaching. With its bright green plumage, enhanced by a rosy chest and throat, this parrot is often trapped for the exotic pet trade. It once lived throughout Cuba, but now it is found only in the eastern forests and on the Isla de la Juventud.

Cuba's National Bird

The plumage of the tocororo, or Cuban trogon, has blue, white, and red feathers, the colors of the Cuban flag. For this reason, it has been chosen as Cuba's national bird. Some people say that it was selected for another reason as well: The tocororo cannot survive in captivity, and its love of freedom mirrors the spirit of the Cuban people. The tocororo is endemic to Cuba, and it is common throughout the island. Its Cuban name, tocororo, is an imitation of its call.

Creatures That Creep and Crawl

Cuba's rain forests and coastal wetlands are the habitat for hundreds of species of snakes, lizards, frogs, and toads. They

More than 180 species of butterflies live in Cuba, including the malachite butterfly.

are also home to swarms of insects, vast colonies of ants, dazzling butterflies, and colorful beetles.

The Cuban boa can reach a length of 15 feet (5 m). Despite its size, this snake does not pose a threat to human beings. A full-grown boa chiefly eats hutias and large lizards.

The endemic Cuban crocodile is considered a critically endangered species. The last surviving specimens live in the

When they are young, Cuban boas live primarily in trees. After they reach adulthood, they tend to stay on the ground, finding shelter under rocks or in holes.

Zapata Swamp and on the Isla de la Juventud. A large male may grow to a length of 11 feet (3.5 m), but most are smaller. These crocodiles eat fish, small mammals, and turtles, which they crush with their strong back teeth. The crocodile can push with its tail to leap from the water and grab animals and birds from overhanging branches.

The Cuban tree frog is found throughout the Caribbean region. At 3 to 5 inches in length (7.5 to 13 cm), it is the largest tree frog in North America. It eats insects, spiders, and smaller tree frogs. Sticky pads on its feet make this tree frog an agile climber. It has been known to climb utility poles and cause power outages by crawling into switch boxes.

When hunting, Cuban crocodiles tend to float in the water. They then leap from the water to ambush prey.

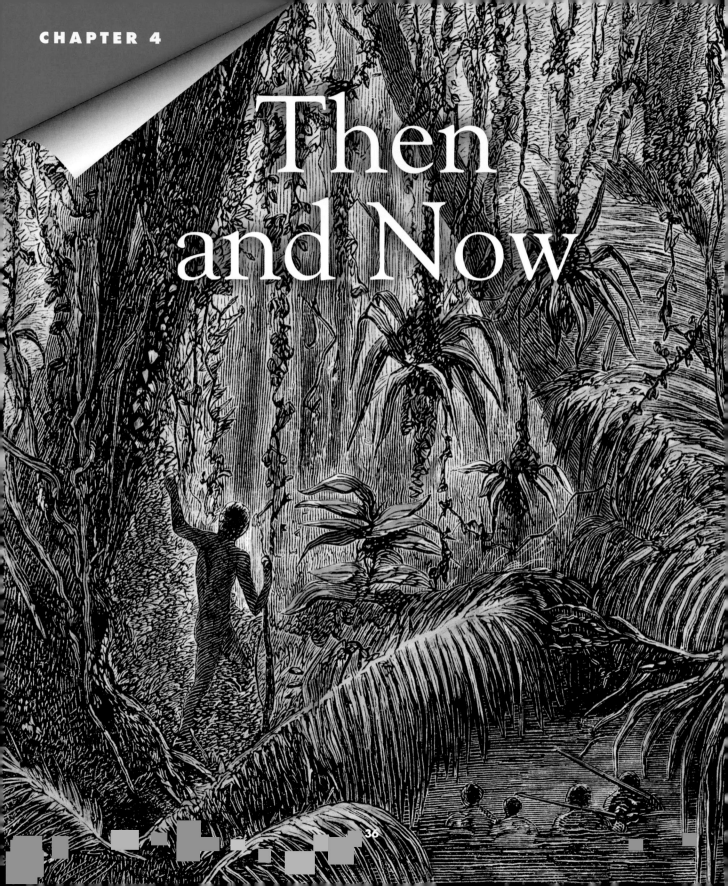

CHAPTER 4

Then and Now

IN A CAVE IN THE VALLEY OF CUBA'S LEVISA RIVER in eastern Cuba, archaeologists have discovered traces of Cuba's earliest inhabitants. People occupied the Levisa Rock Shelter and nearby caves for more than two thousand years, from about 4200 to 2000 BCE. Most archaeologists believe that these early people came from the area in Central America that is the nation of Belize today. The early cave dwellers made knives, hammers, and other tools out of stone. Later they began to make tools and jewelry from shells.

By the fifteenth century, Arawak people, members of related groups who lived throughout the Caribbean, swept into Cuba. The Taíno, as these newcomers are known, built villages around a central square or plaza protected by walls of earth and stones.

A Taíno fisher may have been the first person in Cuba to spot a huge ship with sails like the wings of a monstrous bird. Not in his most dreadful nightmares could he have imagined the horror that lay ahead. The strangers who clambered ashore from the tall ship would change the life of his people forever.

Opposite: **The native people of Cuba gathered food and hunted in the rain forest.**

A Hunger for Wealth

In 1492 Christopher Columbus landed in Cuba, sailing under the flag of Spain. Columbus did not understand that he had reached a region never before seen by Europeans. He believed he had found a new route to India on the Asian continent. Therefore, he called the native people Indians, a mistake that echoes to this day.

Columbus was greatly impressed with the peacefulness of the Taíno people. "So ignorant of arms are they that they grasp swords by the blade," he wrote in his journal. "They are very gentle, not knowing what evil is."

Nevertheless, Columbus remained focused on his mission. The king and queen of Spain had sent him to bring riches to the Spanish crown. When he returned to Spain, Columbus promised to provide "as many slaves as your majesties can command to be shipped, along with as much gold as you need."

The Spaniards sought gold, and they were disappointed that Cuba held little of the precious metal. Instead of gold, they found a generous climate and rich, fertile soil. To work the soil, the Spanish used a system, called *encomienda*, that they had set up throughout their colonies in the Americas. Under this system, each Spaniard was given control of a number of

Early Settlements

- Early Spanish settlement • TAÍNO Native group

native people who would be forced to work the land. Thus, the Taínos and Cuba's other native peoples became the property of the Spanish landowners. The encomienda system reduced native Cubans to the status of slaves. Spaniards justified this forced labor by claiming that their priests were teaching the Indians to become Christians.

Spaniards had built their first settlement in Cuba in 1511. Wherever they went, they enslaved or murdered the Taínos. One Spaniard, a Catholic friar named Bartolomé de Las Casas, described the tragic fate of a Taíno village: "[The Spaniards] set upon the Indians, slashing and slaughtering, until their blood ran like a river."

Christopher Columbus meets the native people of Cuba. Columbus made two journeys to Cuba, in 1492 and again in 1494.

Hatuey and the Kingdom of Heaven

In eastern Cuba, Taíno resistance against the invaders was led by a chieftain called Hatuey. After a brave fight, Hatuey was captured and sentenced to be burned at the stake. A Spanish priest offered to baptize Hatuey, claiming that he might enter the Kingdom of Heaven after his death. Hatuey asked if there were Spaniards in Heaven. The priest said that indeed there were. Upon hearing this, Hatuey refused baptism. He said he did not want to go to paradise if even one Spaniard lived there.

The Taínos fought back, but they had no chance against soldiers who wore metal armor and carried iron swords. The Spaniards rode horses, powerful beasts that the Taínos had never seen before. And they carried weapons they did not know they possessed—diseases such as smallpox and measles. Europeans had been exposed to these diseases for generations, and the Spaniards were largely immune to them. The native people of Cuba, however, had not been exposed to these diseases before, so they had no immunities against them, and they died in shocking numbers.

The Changing Colony

The first enslaved Africans arrived in Cuba as early as 1517. The Africans worked in the fields side by side with the native Cubans. The people of Africa had had contact with Europeans for generations, so unlike the native Cubans, they had acquired immunities to most European diseases. As the native Cubans died off, more and more African slaves were imported.

In the 1520s, the island of Cuba served as a staging area for the Spanish conquest of the Caribbean and Mexico, as well as much of Central and South America. Hernán Cortés lived in Cuba for several years before he conquered Mexico and its Aztec rulers. Because it had the gold and silver that the Spaniards craved, Mexico became the centerpiece of the Spanish Empire in the New World. Cuba and other islands in the Caribbean were relegated to second place in the Spanish imagination.

Havana, with its superb harbor, was the leading city in colonial Cuba. Other early cities included Baracoa, Bayamo,

The Spanish founded Havana in the early 1500s. The city grew quickly as it became a major port where ships stopped to take on supplies.

Trinidad, Sancti Spíritus, and Santiago de Cuba. At first the seat of government was at Santiago de Cuba, but eventually Havana became the colony's capital.

Pirates attack a Spanish ship in the 1600s.

Cuba developed slowly in the 1600s and 1700s. Every few years, hurricanes battered the island, ruining crops and toppling buildings. Pirates lurked off Cuba's shores, waiting to attack gold-laden ships that stopped at the island for supplies of food and water. Foul weather and pirate raids discouraged Spanish settlement in Cuba. For centuries Cuba was a backwater colony in the vast Spanish Empire.

The Ever-Faithful Island

Revolutions rocked Spanish America in the early 1800s. A Catholic priest named Miguel Hidalgo y Costilla led a movement in Mexico that achieved independence after a bloody ten-year war. In the 1820s, Simón Bolívar of Venezuela led successful wars of independence in Bolivia, Venezuela, Colombia,

Aponte's Book of Drawings

In January 1812, a group of enslaved people on plantations near Puerto Príncipe in east-central Cuba rose up and murdered their white masters. Over the next several months, other slave uprisings broke out across the island. Whites in Cuba lived in terror day and night. Officials finally traced the rebellion to a free black man named José Antonio Aponte. In his house outside Havana they found a book of drawings that Aponte had used to inspire his followers. Although the book has never been found, it is said to have included maps of Havana's streets and military forts, pictures of African kings, depictions of incidents in Aponte's life, and even a drawing of U.S. president George Washington. After weeks of questioning, Aponte was beheaded. His head was put on public display to serve as a warning to future rebels.

Ecuador, and Peru. Farther south, José de San Martín helped liberate Argentina and Chile.

Spain had ruled its colonies in the Western Hemisphere for more than three hundred years. Now, within a decade, Spanish power crumbled. Only Cuba and the island of Puerto Rico remained in Spanish hands.

By the middle of the nineteenth century, 36 percent of all Cubans were enslaved people of African descent. During a period of just fifty-one years, from 1816 to 1867, some 595,000 Africans were imported to Cuba.

White Cubans lived in constant fear of slave revolt. They were well aware that a black man named Toussaint Louverture had led a successful uprising against Haiti's French colonists, which resulted in the establishment of the first black-controlled nation in the Caribbean. Cuba's landowners shuddered at the thought that such a thing could happen in Cuba. Though they chafed under colonial rule, they clung to Spain for support and protection. Cuba earned the nickname "the ever-faithful island."

Striving for Freedom

Nevertheless, the spirit of independence burned in many Cuban hearts. In 1868 a wealthy planter named Carlos de Céspedes helped spark a rebellion. The revolutionaries demanded independence from Spain and the abolition of slavery. The resulting conflict, known as the Ten Years' War, raged from 1868 to 1878. At the close of the Ten Years' War, Spanish authorities agreed to end slavery gradually. However, they refused to grant independence to Cuba.

In 1868, Carlos de Céspedes, a wealthy sugar mill owner, proclaimed Cuban independence and freed his slaves, asking them to join him in the fight against Spain.

Slavery officially came to an end in 1886, but the struggle for independence dragged on. Spain did not have the power to quench the independence movement, but the revolutionaries did not have the strength to defeat the Spanish forces.

In 1895, the poet and journalist José Martí led a new surge of warfare. Born in Havana, Martí was a lifelong advocate of Cuban independence. He had spent many years in the United States, and he admired the freedoms ensured by the U.S. Constitution. At the same time, he viewed the United States with suspicion. He knew that wealthy Americans coveted Cuba's sugar and coffee plantations.

Thousands of Cubans died in the uprising that Martí inspired. José Martí himself was killed in the Battle of Dos Ríos on May 19, 1895. He is remembered today as a national hero.

A Cuban sugar plantation. In the mid-1800s, sugar became a major part of the Cuban economy, and by 1860, Cuba was producing almost one-third of all the sugar in the world.

The Spanish-American War

Many Americans lived in Cuba during the late nineteenth century. A number of powerful fruit, sugar, and coffee companies urged the U.S. government to purchase Cuba from Spain. As Cuba's war for independence raged, U.S. newspapers ran stories about Spain's atrocities. Many of these stories exaggerated the situation in an attempt to excite the public and sell more papers. Such reporting came to be known as "yellow journalism." In one sensational story about the Spanish general Valeriano Weyler, a headline in the *New York Journal* blared, "Weyler Throws Nuns into Prison. Butcher Wages Brutal Warfare on Helpless Women."

In 1898, U.S. president William McKinley sent the Battleship *Maine* to Havana Harbor. At the time, revolutionaries were battling almost constantly with the Spanish military. McKinley hoped the battleship, with a contingent of marines on board, would protect the U.S. citizens who lived and owned businesses in Cuba. On February 15, 1898, the *Maine* exploded and sank in Havana Harbor. In the disaster, 261 Americans lost their lives.

To this day the cause of the explosion remains a mystery. Some people now suspect that a fire in the ship's kitchen triggered the blast. But in 1898, newspapers claimed that the battleship was sunk by the Spanish navy, and the U.S. press demanded war. In April 1898, the United States declared war on Spain. Prompted by the yellow press, a battle cry rang out: "Remember the *Maine*!"

The Spanish-American War was over quickly. It lasted only four months, from April to August 1898. Early in the war an American fleet set up a blockade to prevent Cuban ships from leaving Havana Harbor. Meanwhile, U.S. troops landed at Santiago. Spanish forces on both land and sea were weak and disorganized, and resistance was meager.

The war ended with the Treaty of Paris, signed on December 10, 1898. Spain ceded Guam, Puerto Rico, and the Philippines to the United States. U.S. forces occupying Cuba were given temporary control of the island until Cuba was granted its independence in 1902.

The Hero of San Juan Hill

The best-known American participant in the Spanish-American War was Theodore Roosevelt. As a young army colonel, Roosevelt led a cavalry unit nicknamed the Rough Riders up San Juan Hill near Santiago to storm a Spanish fort. Victory in the battle helped make Roosevelt famous. The story of his heroism launched him on a path that led to the White House. Roosevelt later said, "San Juan was the greatest day of my life."

Freedom in Name Only

The island of Cuba was not really free. From 1898 until 1902, a U.S. occupying army was stationed on the island. Cuba ratified a constitution in 1901, and officially became an independent nation in 1902. However, the following year, Cuba and the United States signed a treaty leasing land at Guantánamo Bay to the United States to use as a naval base. To this day, Guantánamo Bay remains in U.S. hands.

U.S. troops camp near Havana in 1906. In the early 1900s, the United States frequently intervened in Cuban affairs.

Conquest of a Disease

For centuries yellow fever ravaged Cuba. The disease, which attacks the victim's liver and turns the skin yellow, can result in death. A Cuban doctor named Carlos Finlay believed that yellow fever was spread by mosquitoes. Doctors from the United States agreed and launched large-scale mosquito control programs in Cuba. The U.S. occupation of Cuba led to the defeat of yellow fever.

The Cuban constitution contained a controversial provision called the Platt Amendment. The amendment stated that the United States had the right to intervene in Cuba if revolutionary conflict flared anew. In effect, the Platt Amendment gave the United States license to invade Cuba any time American leaders saw fit. The Cuban general Juan Gualberto Gómez proclaimed, "The Platt Amendment has reduced the independence and sovereignty of the Cuban Republic to a myth."

The Platt Amendment and the Guantánamo Bay occupation were examples of a trend some Cubans called "Yankee imperialism." They felt that the United States used its wealth and power to bully its Latin American neighbors. They pointed out that American companies bought Cuban property and businesses. By the 1920s, companies in the United States and other foreign countries owned 80 percent of Cuba's sugar industry. American investors also bought up Cuba's railroads. American tourists flocked to American-run hotels that sprouted up along Cuba's beaches. Cubans held low-paying jobs in the foreign-owned hotels and restaurants. Vacationers commonly spent more on lunch than the waiters and cleaning staff earned in weeks.

Then, in the 1930s, the Great Depression shook the economies of nations around the world. In Cuba, sugar prices dropped, and as income declined unrest grew. With the country in growing turmoil, a group of army sergeants overthrew the Cuban government. This 1933 "Sergeants Revolt" was led by Sergeant Fulgencio Batista, who became a major force in Cuban politics in the years after the coup. Batista was elected president in 1940. During his presidency, he expanded education and the Cuban economy grew. He left office in 1944 but then became president again following a coup in 1952. This time, he ruled as a dictator who brutally put down his opponents.

The United States tolerated Batista's rule because he was anticommunist. Most American political and business leaders hated communism, the idea that the government should own factories and farms so that all people would share in their profits. The gap between rich and poor had grown wide in Cuba, however, and the idea appealed to some people there. The time was ripe for revolution.

Revolution

Fidel Castro was born in 1926 near the Cuban town of Mayarí, in eastern Cuba. His father was a wealthy sugarcane farmer who had immigrated from Spain. Although Castro lived in comfort as a youth, his neighbors struggled in poverty. This difference between rich and poor became the central issue in Castro's life.

In 1945, Castro entered the University of Havana, where he studied law. After graduating, he became involved in politics. He planned to run for election to Congress in 1952, but before he had

Cuban Revolution

Havana
Yaguajay (Dec. 19–30, 1958)
Santa Clara (Dec. 28, 1958–Jan. 1, 1959)
Caribbean Sea
Castro brothers arrive on the *Granma* Dec. 2, 1956
Las Mercedes (July 29–Aug. 8, 1958)
La Plata (July 11–21, 1958)
Moncada Barracks (July 26, 1953)

✳ Battle ⟵ Route of revolutionaries

the chance, Batista overthrew the president and canceled the elections. Castro believed that to change Cuba, Batista would have to go.

On July 26, 1953, Castro led an assault on the Moncada Barracks in Santiago de Cuba. He had gathered an army of shoeshine boys and parking lot attendants. Castro hoped to storm the military barracks and make off with the weapons stored inside. He viewed this attack as the first battle in a new Cuban revolution.

The assault failed miserably. Castro was captured and sent to prison. But the operation against the Moncada Barracks put Castro in the public eye. Among the nation's poor he became known as a bold revolutionary.

Castro was released from prison after two years. He and his brother, Raúl, went to Mexico, where they formed the 26th of July Movement. The movement was named for the ill-fated attack on the Moncada Barracks. In December 1956, Castro and about eighty followers returned to Cuba, vowing to overthrow Batista's government. Their ship, the yacht *Granma*, landed at Playa de las Coloradas near the town of Niquero, in southeastern Cuba, on December 2, 1956.

Only three days after the *Granma* landed, most of the rebels were killed or captured. But Fidel and Raúl Castro, with a band of less than twenty men, escaped to the Sierra Maestra mountains in the interior. With them was a passionate revo-

In 1959, demonstrators gathered in front of the presidential palace in Havana to show their support for the Cuban Revolution.

lutionary from Argentina named Che Guevara. From their mountain hideouts, the Castros' forces waged stealthy guerrilla warfare. They blew up bridges, destroyed railroad tracks, and captured military supplies. News of each successful raid was broadcast over a secret radio network operated by the Castro brothers. More and more of Cuba's poor people began to support Castro and his movement to overthrow Batista.

On New Year's Day, 1959, Batista fled the country. A week later, Fidel Castro and the other revolutionaries swept into Havana. Castro now led the island nation. People celebrated in the streets.

Meanwhile, the United States looked on warily. Castro was sympathetic to the communist cause. He came to power at the height of the Cold War, the struggle for influence between the United States and the Union of Soviet Socialist Republics, or USSR, a large communist nation in eastern Europe and Asia that has since disintegrated, leaving Russia and more than

Hero of the Revolution

Born in Argentina, Ernesto (Che) Guevara (1928–1967) traveled widely in Latin America when he was a medical student. He was shocked by the poverty he saw and became convinced that a communist revolution was the only hope. Guevara met Fidel and Raúl Castro in Mexico City and joined them in their effort to overthrow Fulgencio Batista in Cuba. After Castro came to power, Guevara helped launch Cuba's land reform and literacy programs. In 1965, he left Cuba to work in other countries, including Czechoslovakia and Congo. He was killed in Bolivia just two years later.

a dozen other countries in its place. Would Castro establish a communist nation just 90 miles (145 km) from American shores and form an alliance with the USSR?

Thousands of wealthy Cubans, fearing violence, fled Cuba and took up residence in the United States, chiefly in Florida. Castro passed laws to break up large farms and redistribute the land to peasants. He also took over American-owned sugar-refining plants. Shortly after taking power, Castro ordered more than five hundred of Batista's followers to be executed.

Celia Sánchez, Revolutionary

Among the many women who helped launch the Cuban Revolution was Celia Sánchez (1920–1980). She helped plan the landing of the *Granma* and later supplied the guerrillas with food, medicine, and weapons. She also carried messages to the fighters, hiding them in a white ginger lily that became her insignia.

Between December 1960 and October 1962, more than fourteen thousand Cuban children and teens arrived in the United States, unaccompanied by their parents. Operation Peter Pan, as this exodus of Cuban children was called, was sponsored by the Catholic Welfare Bureau under the direction of a young priest in Miami, Florida, named Bryan O. Walsh. Some of the children had relatives they could stay with in the United States, but many others were scattered among foster homes in thirty states. The Cuban parents sent their children to the United States because they believed they would have better lives there. The parents feared that if their children remained in Cuba they would not be safe and they might be brainwashed into following communism, which the schools were reformed to promote.

Alarmed by the events taking place so close to home, the United States broke off diplomatic relations with Cuba. It also enacted a strict trade embargo. Under the embargo the United States would no longer buy any goods from Cuba. Until that

Following the revolution, the Cuban government established an ambitious literacy program. In three years, the literacy rate rose from between 60 and 70 percent to 96 percent. Most of the people who benefited from this program were poor farmers (right).

The Alzados

During the Cuban Revolution, as the government seized property, many Cuban farmers fought a guerrilla war against the Castro forces. In a reversal of roles, the rebel farmers took to the mountains, much as Castro had done in earlier years, and fought the Cuban army. The farmers fighting for their land called themselves the Alzados, from a Spanish word meaning "to rise." The Cuban government waged war against the Alzados from 1959 to 1965, until Castro's forces finally eliminated the rebels. The Cuban government called the conflict with the Alzados the War Against the Bandits.

time, the United States had been the biggest market for Cuba's sugar. Eventually, Cuba developed trading partnerships with the Soviet Union and several nations in Eastern Europe.

Working in secrecy, the U.S. government hatched plans to overthrow or even murder Fidel Castro. The U.S. Central Intelligence Agency (CIA) held meetings with mobsters whose casinos had been taken over by the Cuban government. Government agents and mobsters discussed the possibility of assassinating the Cuban leader.

Crisis

In April 1961, an army of about 1,300 men landed at the Bay of Pigs in Cuba. The men were Cuban exiles, most of whom had recently fled the revolution. They intended to overthrow the Castro government. At first, American officials claimed the United States had nothing to do with the invasion. However, that claim was a lie. The landings were planned under the administration of President Dwight D. Eisenhower and carried out by order of President John F. Kennedy, who had taken office only three months earlier. At the last moment, Kennedy canceled plans to support the landings with protection from U.S. aircraft.

Without air cover, the invasion was a complete disaster. All of the invaders were killed or captured. When it was obvious that the attack had failed, Kennedy reluctantly admitted that his country had backed the Bay of Pigs operation.

The U.S. defeat at the Bay of Pigs made Fidel Castro an even greater hero in the eyes of the Cuban people. Here at last was a leader with the strength to stand up to the United States.

Riding a wave of popularity, Castro proclaimed Cuba to be a communist nation. He sent his brother, Raúl, to the USSR to meet with Soviet leader Nikita Khrushchev. Raúl Castro told Khrushchev that he and his brother feared the United States would again invade Cuban shores. Khrushchev offered to put nuclear-armed missiles in Cuba to deter another invasion. The Castro government accepted the plan.

Cuban soldiers fire on invaders at the Bay of Pigs in 1961. One hundred eighteen of the invading forces were killed, and another 1,202 were captured.

The Cuban negotiations in the USSR were held in strict secrecy. At the time, the Soviet Union and the United States maintained a tense standoff. There was a delicate balance of power, with each of the two superpowers commanding a deadly arsenal of missiles. Although the Soviet Union had few long-range missiles capable of crossing the ocean and striking targets in the United States, it did have many intermediate-range missiles accurate at distances of 1,000 to 2,000 miles (1,600 to 3,200 km). The missile deal with the Castro government allowed the Soviets to deploy intermediate-range missiles aimed at the United States from Cuba, thus upsetting the delicate balance of power.

Fidel Castro (left) hugs Soviet leader Nikita Khrushchev during a meeting in 1960.

Cuban exiles in the United States watch President John F. Kennedy discuss the Cuban Missile Crisis in October 1962.

After the failed Bay of Pigs invasion, the United States regularly sent U-2 surveillance planes over Cuba. The U-2 was America's "eye in the sky." The plane flew too high to be shot down by antiaircraft guns or enemy aircraft, yet it carried cameras sensitive enough to photograph objects as small as cars on the ground below. In the fall of 1962, a series of U-2 photographs revealed Soviet ships coming and going in Cuban ports.

An espionage flight on October 14, 1962, confirmed America's gravest fears. A photo revealed that the Soviets were moving missile-launching equipment into Cuba. Once operational, a fleet of missiles in Cuba could obliterate the entire eastern half of the United States and kill millions of Americans.

On October 22, 1962, President Kennedy made a televised speech to warn the world about the weapons buildup in Cuba. "It shall be the policy of this nation," Kennedy declared, "to regard any nuclear missile launched from Cuba against any nation in the Western Hemisphere as an attack by the Soviet Union on the United States, requiring a full retaliatory response on the Soviet Union."

For the next six days the world held its breath as nuclear war loomed. The island nation of Cuba was the focus of this global tension, but the Cuban people and their leader, Fidel Castro, had no control over the circumstances. Only Soviet officers could give the order to launch missiles. Cuba was a pawn in the great confrontation known ever after as the Cuban Missile Crisis.

A U.S. naval ship (gray) escorts a Soviet ship carrying missiles out of Cuba at the end of the Cuban Missile Crisis.

Calm heads finally won the day. Premier Khrushchev withdrew the Russian missiles from Cuba and President Kennedy ordered his military to stand down. Kennedy agreed not to invade Cuba. Both sides claimed victory in the crisis.

Facing the Challenges

In the years after the communist revolution, Cuba looked to the Soviet Union for help. Soviet money and know-how kept the Cuban economy afloat. The Cuban government provided free schools for children, literacy classes for adults, and free medical care for Cubans of all ages. In return, all Cubans were

People of all backgrounds gathered to cut sugarcane during harvesttime.

Fidel Castro speaks to a massive crowd in Havana's Revolution Square in 1965.

expected to support the revolution. At harvesttime, teachers, office workers, and engineers left their regular jobs and went to the farms to cut sugarcane or pick fruit.

Few people went hungry in Cuba, but meals were simple and monotonous. Stores stocked only the most basic household items. There were no fancy toys or clothes. Few people could afford automobiles. Over and over Castro promised that life would get better as the revolution moved to its next phase. Cubans waited hopefully for better days to come.

Some people had no such hope. They wanted to leave the island. Hundreds of thousands of people emigrated to the United States. Many doctors and engineers left. Castro restricted travel because he feared that more of the country's valuable professionals would flee, thus causing Cuba to suffer a "brain drain."

A boat full of Cuban immigrants heads for Florida during the Mariel Boatlift.

In the fall of 1980, Castro's government suddenly eased restrictions on travel. Thousands of Cubans crowded into Mariel Harbor near Havana, hoping to catch boats to the United States. This mass migration, known as the Mariel Boatlift, became another clash between Cuba and the U.S. government. At first, U.S. president Jimmy Carter welcomed the Cuban émigrés. Then U.S. officials discovered that Castro had released prison inmates and psychiatric patients among the many people who left Cuba. In October 1980, the mass emigration came to an end. By that time, about 125,000 Cubans had settled on American shores.

In 1991, the Soviet Union collapsed, and Soviet aid to Cuba ended abruptly. The Cuban people suffered shortages of food, fuel, and medicine. These years of hardship, from 1991 to the late 1990s, are known in Cuba as the Special Period in a Time of Peace.

Recent Times

By 2006, the year he turned eighty, Fidel Castro's health had declined. In 2008, his younger brother, Raúl, assumed leadership. By this time, communism had disappeared from most

Raúl Castro was the head of the Cuban armed forces for forty-nine years before taking over the presidency from his brother in 2008. During much of that time, he was also the first vice president of Cuba.

places around the world. Nevertheless, Cuba remained a communist nation, one of only a handful of communist economies in the world.

Cuba's economy was lagging, so the country began to make changes. People were allowed to start their own small businesses. The government started taking a less active role in agriculture and construction, and many government employees were laid off. The nation eased restrictions on Cubans traveling to foreign countries.

Many buildings in Cuba fell into disrepair in the years after the revolution.

During this time of change, many Cubans hoped to improve relations with the United States. The U.S. trade embargo had been in place for more than fifty years, but rather than bringing down the communist regime, it had harmed the people of Cuba. In 2013, the United States and Cuba began negotiating in secret. In December 2014, U.S. president Barack Obama announced that the United States was reestablishing diplomatic relations with Cuba and planned to reopen its embassy in Havana. He hoped to lift the trade embargo, though that requires approval by Congress.

Many Cuban exiles in the United States were outraged by the changes. They argued that the Cuban government oppresses its people and felt betrayed by the U.S. government's decision. However, most people in Cuba are hopeful that these changes might lead to a better future.

A group of teenagers in Havana. Many Cubans believe that improved relations between Cuba and the United States will bring them greater prosperity.

CHAPTER 5

The Power of the Party

O<small>N</small> M<small>AY</small> 1 <small>EACH YEAR, THOUSANDS OF</small> C<small>UBANS</small> fill Revolution Square in Havana to celebrate the holiday known as Labor Day. They carry banners, sing patriotic songs, and listen to speeches by political leaders. Labor Day is celebrated in many of the world's nations, but in Cuba it holds a place of special importance. It celebrates the worker and the Communist Party, the only political party in Cuba.

Opposite: **More than half a million people took part in the Labor Day parade in Havana in 2014.**

Under the Constitution

The current constitution of the Republic of Cuba went into effect on February 24, 1976. The constitution calls for a strong central government controlled by the Communist Party of Cuba (the Partido Comunista de Cuba, or PCC). According to the constitution, the PCC is "the highest leading force of society and the state." The head of the party, and the country, is the president, currently Raúl Castro.

The constitution divides Cuba's government into three main branches. The legislative branch is composed of the National Assembly of People's Power and the Council of State. The Council of Ministers comprises the executive branch. The judicial branch, or court system, is headed by the People's Supreme Court.

The National Assembly

Members of the National Assembly applaud a speech by President Raúl Castro.

Cuba's parliament, the National Assembly of People's Power, is composed of roughly six hundred members who are elected to five-year terms. It meets twice a year, and each session lasts

only for a few days. The National Assembly elects thirty-one of its members to form the Council of State, which handles the duties of the National Assembly when it is not in session. The National Assembly also appoints the Council of Ministers.

The National Assembly has the power to amend the constitution; pass, amend, and repeal laws; approve plans for economic development; and work out domestic and foreign

Chinese president Hu Jintau and Cuban president Raúl Castro watch officials sign a treaty between their two countries in the Council of State.

Voting

All Cuban citizens age sixteen and over are eligible to vote. The government puts a huge amount of pressure on Cubans to vote. As a result, the voter turnout in Cuba is very high compared to that in many other countries. In most Cuban elections, as many as 99 percent of all voters go to the polls.

The Power of the Party **69**

The Hymn of Bayamo

Cuba's national anthem, "The Hymn of Bayamo," was composed in 1868 by Perucho Figueredo. Figueredo fought against Spain in the Battle of Bayamo and composed the song on horseback. He was executed by the Spanish in 1870. As he faced the firing squad, he shouted a line from the song, "¡Morir por la patria es vivir!" (To die for one's country is to live!) The song has served as Cuba's national anthem since 1902.

Spanish lyrics

Al combate corred bayameses,
Que la patria os contempla orgullosa.
No temáis una muerte gloriosa,
Que morir por la patria es vivir.

En cadenas vivir es morir,
En afrenta y oprobio sumidos.
Del clarín escuchad el sonido,
A las armas, valientes, corred.

English translation

Hasten to battle, men of Bayamo,
For the homeland looks to you proudly.
You do not fear a glorious death,
For to die for your country is to live.

To live in chains
Is to live in dishonor and shame.
Hear the clarion call.
Hasten, brave ones, to battle.

policies. It elects the members of the Supreme Court and the attorney general's office.

When the National Assembly is not in session, the Council of State passes and interprets laws. On the president's request, it has the power to replace the members of the Council of Ministers. It also gives instructions to the courts through the governing council of the People's Supreme Court.

Raúl Castro wields great power in Cuba. He is the president of the Council of State, president of the Council of Ministers, first secretary of the Communist Party, and commander in chief of the armed forces.

The Council of Ministers

The leader of Cuba serves both as president of the Council of State and president of the Council of Ministers. The Council of Ministers is the nation's highest government body. Members of the Council of Ministers are nominated by the National Assembly of People's Power, which includes the president, the first vice president, and the vice presidents of the Council of Ministers itself.

The Council of Ministers enforces the policies established by the People's Assembly and the Council of State. It proposes domestic and foreign policy plans and sees that they are carried out once they are passed by the People's Assembly.

The Court System

The highest court in Cuba is the People's Supreme Court. Members of the court are elected by the National Assembly. Each of Cuba's provinces has a provincial court, whose judges are elected by the provincial assembly. Judges of the municipal courts are elected by the municipal assemblies. Several specialized courts function as parts of the People's Supreme Court. They include the Whole Court, the State Council, Crimes-Against-the-State Court, military courts, and criminal, civil, and labor courts.

Cuba's National Government

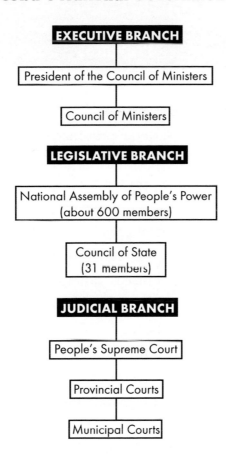

EXECUTIVE BRANCH

President of the Council of Ministers

Council of Ministers

LEGISLATIVE BRANCH

National Assembly of People's Power
(about 600 members)

Council of State
(31 members)

JUDICIAL BRANCH

People's Supreme Court

Provincial Courts

Municipal Courts

Provinces

Provinces and Municipalities

Cuba is divided into sixteen provinces. The largest of the provinces by area is Camagüey, and the smallest is Isla de la Juventud. Each of Cuba's provinces is governed by a provincial assembly of at least seventy-five members. The provincial assembly elects a provincial committee. The president of the provincial committee is the leading official in the province, but the provincial committees do not have the money or power to do much. Instead, the Communist Party plays a large role in the local government.

Each of Cuba's 169 municipalities, which are like counties in the United States, is governed by a municipal assembly. Like the National Assembly and the provincial assemblies, each municipal assembly elects a municipal committee. The president of the municipal committee functions as mayor.

Havana, Cuba's Capital

Founded in 1515, Havana, or La Habana, is one of the oldest capitals in the Americas. With approximately 2,163,824 people, it is the largest city in Cuba and in the entire Caribbean region. Havana is the political and financial center of Cuba. It is a major port and a center of manufacturing for such products as medicines and chemicals, and for food processing.

Havana is built around a harbor on Cuba's northwest coast. The Morro Castle, or Castillo del Morro, has guarded the harbor since the 1600s. Completed in 1577, the Castillo de la Real Fuerza, or Castle of the Royal Force, is the oldest stone fort in the Americas. Its west tower is crowned by a bronze weathervane in the form of a woman called La Giraldilla. The figure is a symbol of the city. In 2010, the fort opened as a mari-

time museum. On the main floor stands a huge model of the *Santísima Trinidad*, which was first launched in 1769 and became the largest ship in the world after it was remodeled in 1796.

The dome of the Old National Capitol (above) dominates Havana's skyline. The building, completed in 1929, was designed to resemble the U.S. Capitol in Washington, D.C. Today, the building is the headquarters of the Cuban Academy of Sciences.

Another prominent landmark is the José Martí Memorial, which stands 358 feet (109 m) above the streets. The monument is a tower in the form of a five-pointed star. At the base of the tower is a colossal statue of José Martí, Cuba's national hero.

Havana also has many fine museums. The National Museum of Fine Arts houses an extensive collection of Cuban painting and sculpture from the colonial era to the present. A sister museum, the Asturian Center, displays European art and the art of ancient civilizations.

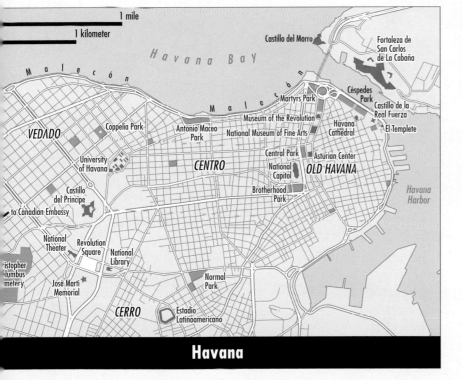

Havana

CHAPTER 6

Waiting in Line

ACCORDING TO AN OLD CUBAN JOKE, FIDEL Castro once sent a spy to study the living conditions in the United States. When the spy returned, he reported, "Those people are way, way behind us! They're still eating foods we haven't bothered with in years—steak, milk shakes, and buttered toast!" The Cuban people have grown accustomed to living simply, but every day they hear promises that better times are coming. No matter what happens, they retain their sense of humor.

The State-Run Economy

After the revolution of 1959, Fidel Castro set up tight government control over the nation's economy. His goal was to reduce the gap between rich and poor, to ensure that all Cubans would be equals. In Castro's state-run economy, nearly all farms and factories were operated by the government. About 91 percent of all Cuban workers were government employees.

Until 1990, Cuba's economy received major support from the Soviet Union. When the Soviet Union collapsed, that critical support disappeared. Cuba plummeted into a time of hardship known as the Special Period in a Time of Peace. To reverse the disastrous downturn, Castro revived a once flourishing industry: tourism. Crumbling hotels and restaurants were refurbished, and glistening new resorts sprang up. Once again, foreigners flocked to Cuba's beaches, bringing millions of desperately needed dollars to the Cuban economy. Most of the tourists came from Canada and Europe. The U.S. government did not permit American citizens to visit Cuba without a special reason such as for education or research.

A carriage transports tourists through historic Havana. More than 2.5 million foreign tourists arrive in the country every year. The largest number is from Canada.

A woman sells fruit and
vegetables at her own
produce stand in Havana.

In the 1990s, changes began to be made in the Cuban economy. Cubans are now allowed to obtain permits to start small businesses, such as operating a taxi or setting up a produce stand; to have cell phones; and to buy and sell houses and modern automobiles.

Getting By

The average salary in Cuba is only about US$20 per month. The Cuban government provides some essentials of daily life. Cubans can receive rations of basic foods such as rice, beans, milk, and vegetables. Medical care is free for everyone. Education is also free of charge at every level, from preschool to university. Anyone in Cuba can go to college if his or her grades are good enough.

Cuba's standard currency is the Cuban peso, or CUP. In 1994, Cuba launched a new form of currency, the Cuban convertible peso, or CUC. About 25 CUPs equal one CUC, and one CUC is worth approximately US$1. Most Cubans are paid in CUPs, but most goods in the stores, from soap to soup, are priced in CUCs.

Both CUPs and CUCs come in bills with values of 1, 3, 5, 10, 20, 50, and 100. Each denomination of Cuban peso depicts a major figure from Cuban history on the front of the bill and a scene from Cuban history or culture on the back. For example, the one-peso bill has a portrait of José Martí on the front. The other side shows Fidel Castro and his troops triumphantly entering Havana. The front of each CUC bill shows a monument to a Cuban hero. The backs depict a scene from Cuban history. The 3 CUC bill shows the monument to Che Guevara in the town of Santa Clara on the front and the Battle of Santa Clara during the revolution on the back.

In order to obtain food rations and health care, however, Cubans must deal with a vast government bureaucracy. Always there are forms to fill out, papers to sign, and official stamps to obtain—and there are always long lines. Even to buy bread or bananas, a Cuban must wait patiently behind dozens of other people. *La cola cubana*, the Cuban line, is a way of life.

Goods and Services

Agriculture accounts for about 4 percent of Cuba's gross domestic product (GDP), the total value of the goods and services a country produces. Another 22 percent comes from

manufacturing and mining. About 74 percent of Cuba's GDP comes from the service industries. Services include education, medicine, restaurants, hotels, sales, and much more.

Most people in Cuba, such as this bus driver, work in service industries.

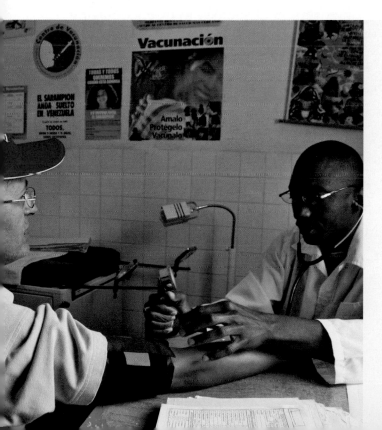

Oil for Doctors

Cuba produces only small amounts of oil, so it imports most of its fuel. Much of its oil comes from the nation of Venezuela, in South America. Cuba pays for some of its oil imports by sending nurses and doctors to volunteer in Venezuela's hospitals and rural clinics.

Cuba also provides thousands of doctors to more than one hundred other countries around the world. Some Cuban medical personnel help when there is a natural disaster or epidemic, while others are part of longstanding programs to provide care in countries where it is needed. In fact, medical workers are among Cuba's most valuable exports.

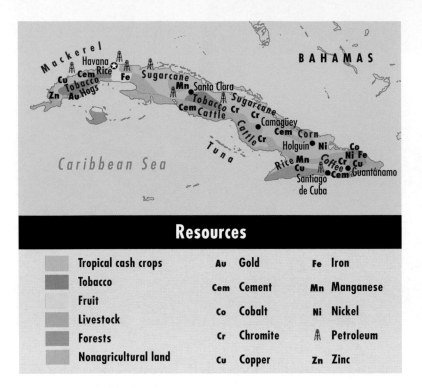

Resources

▨ Tropical cash crops	Au	Gold	Fe	Iron		
▨ Tobacco	Cem	Cement	Mn	Manganese		
▨ Fruit	Co	Cobalt	Ni	Nickel		
▨ Livestock						
▨ Forests	Cr	Chromite	⚒	Petroleum		
▨ Nonagricultural land	Cu	Copper	Zn	Zinc		

Raising Crops

During the Special Period in a Time of Peace that began in 1991, Cuban farmers could not obtain fuel to run their tractors or fertilizer for their crops. Under these extreme conditions, large farms that raised sugarcane, coffee, and other crops for export no longer functioned. Without income from exports, Cubans could not import the food they needed. Millions of people faced starvation.

In 1992, the Cuban government stepped in by encouraging farmers to return to methods that had been used by their grandparents and great-grandparents. Farmers replaced gas-fueled tractors with oxen, and harvesting machinery with machetes. With government support to buy seed and soil, city dwellers created vegetable gardens in empty lots and on rooftops. Since chemical fertilizers were scarce and expensive, Cubans returned to organic farming methods. One observer noted, "[This is] the largest conversion from conventional agriculture to organic or semi-organic farming that the world has ever known."

Sugar remains Cuba's leading agricultural product, although sugar production has been greatly reduced. In 1980, growers produced some 5 million tons of sugarcane. In 2013, only 1.5

million tons of sugarcane were harvested. Cuba's other major crops are tobacco, citrus fruit, coffee, and rice. Cuban farmers also produce cattle, pigs, chickens, and other livestock.

Workers use machetes to harvest sugarcane.

What Cuba Grows, Makes, and Mines

AGRICULTURE (2011)

Sugarcane	15,800,000 metric tons
Tomatoes	601,000 metric tons
Plantains	585,000 metric tons

MANUFACTURING (2009)

Cement	1,677,500 metric tons
Steel	269,000 metric tons
Cigarettes	13,100,000,000 units

MINING (2010)

Nickel	71,000 metric tons
Cobalt	3,600 metric tons

An image of Fidel Castro stands outside the Cuban Steel Company building in Havana.

Industry

Sugar refining is still an important industry in Cuba, although it has declined steeply since the 1990s. Factories also produce petroleum products, steel, cement, and pharmaceuticals.

Cuban Cigars

Cuban cigars are considered to be some of the finest in the world. Only the finest materials are used, and they are made carefully, using techniques that date back hundreds of years. Most of the tobacco used in Cuban cigars grows in Pinar del Río Province, on the western end of Cuba. Rolling the tobacco in the tobacco-leaf wrapping takes great skill. Cigar rollers, or *torcedores*, are highly respected. Due to the U.S. embargo on Cuban goods, Cuban cigars cannot legally be imported into the United States.

In Latin America, Africa, and Asia, Cuba is known for its work in the field of medicines, or pharmaceuticals. Cuba gives major support to its scientists and researchers. It exports many vaccines that help protect people from viral and bacterial diseases. Some research labs in Cuba have made exciting breakthroughs in the development of vaccines against certain types of cancer.

Mines in Cuba produce nickel, cobalt, and sand for cement and other construction materials. Deposits of gold have been discovered on the Isla de la Juventud. In 2012, drilling began in offshore oil fields along Cuba's northern coast. Companies in India, Spain, and Norway show interest in helping Cuba develop its petroleum resources.

A worker cuts slices of limestone at a quarry near Matanzas, in northern Cuba.

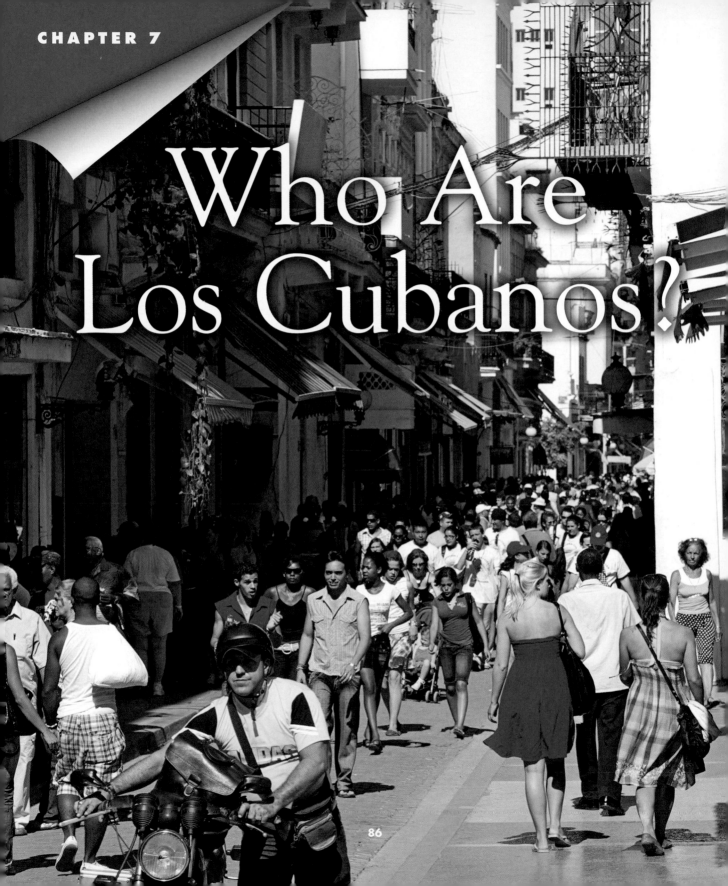

CHAPTER 7

Who Are Los Cubanos?

WHEN MOST CUBANS DESCRIBE THEMSELVES, they put their country first. "*¡Yo soy cubano!*" (I am Cuban!) they say proudly. But if you inquire further, you will discover that Cubans come from a medley of ethnic groups. They blend together to build one nation, but each group maintains its own identity and traditions.

Population

In 2014, Cuba had an estimated population of 11,047,251. About 75 percent of all Cuban people are urban dwellers, living in cities or large towns. The rest live on farms or in rural villages.

No accurate assessment of the ethnic background of Cubans exists, and the numbers vary widely. According to one survey, about 64 percent of all Cubans consider themselves white. About 27 percent of Cubans describe themselves as mulattoes, or people of mixed race. Blacks make up 9 percent

Population of Major Cities (2014 est.)	
Havana	2,163,824
Santiago de Cuba	555,865
Camagüey	347,562
Holguín	319,102
Santa Clara	250,512
Guantánamo	272,801

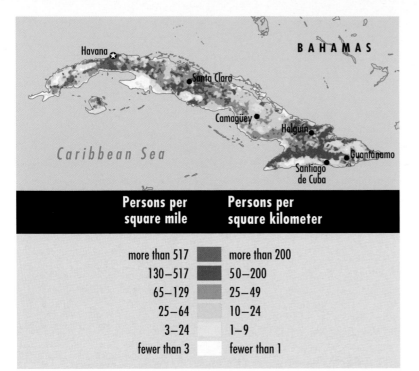

Persons per square mile	Persons per square kilometer
more than 517	more than 200
130–517	50–200
65–129	25–49
25–64	10–24
3–24	1–9
fewer than 3	fewer than 1

Ethnicity in Cuba (2012 est.)

White	64%
Mixed	27%
Black	9%

of Cuba's population. Cuba also has a small Asian population. Many Cubans also have indigenous, or native, ancestors.

Spanish Heritage

Spanish has been the chief language of Cuba since Spain colonized the island in the 1500s. Many of the early colonists came from the Canary Islands, which lie about 1,200 miles (2,000 km) off Spain's Atlantic coast. In the centuries that followed, waves of immigrants came from the Spanish province of Galicia. Thousands of Catalonians from Spain's Pyrenees Mountains also settled in Cuba.

Afro-Cubans

Most Afro-Cubans are the descendants of the millions of enslaved people who were brought to Cuba between 1511 and 1867. Others migrated to Cuba from the neighboring nation of Haiti during the nineteenth and early twentieth centuries.

The largest group of Africans who arrived in Cuba belonged to the Yoruba people. Most lived in West Africa, in what is now Nigeria. Other people came from Africa's northwest coast. Although the Africans in Cuba spoke different

languages and had a variety of customs and religions, they shared the common bond of oppression. They drew together for comfort and support. Over time they came to see themselves as a unified group, the Afro-Cubans.

An Afro-Cuban man in Havana. The capital is home to the highest proportion of Afro-Cubans of any city in the country.

Antonio Maceo, "The Bronze Titan"

Antonio Maceo was a Cuban with both black and white ancestors who rose to the rank of lieutenant general during the Ten Years' War. He was second in command of the *mambises*, or Cuban rebels, in the War for Independence. He was wounded twenty-five times over the years, but miraculously managed to survive. Because of his strength and endurance his men called him the Bronze Titan. Maceo finally received a fatal wound in December 1896. The Cacahual Monument south of Havana marks Maceo's grave and the grave of his loyal lieutenant, Francisco Gómez.

The Last of the Taínos

Centuries of Spanish colonization devastated Cuba's native peoples. By the twentieth century, most historians believed that the Taínos and other native groups had died out completely. However, scientists now have the ability to study a person's genetic makeup and learn about his or her ancestors. They discovered that about 12 percent of all Cubans have some indigenous ancestors. Some five thousand people in the mountains of eastern Cuba are of predominantly Taíno descent.

A Taíno woman in Baracoa, on the eastern tip of Cuba. This region has the largest Taíno population in the country.

The Taíno language has been forgotten. But among the rural people of eastern Cuba, many Taíno customs linger: People plant small, tightly packed vegetable gardens on mounds of earth, just as the Taíno did when Columbus arrived. They also use wild herbs for medicines as their ancestors had done for thousands of years.

Speaking Spanish

Spanish is spoken throughout Cuba. Many Cubans are also fluent in English, because it is taught widely in the schools.

Spanish is a strongly phonetic language, which means that it is generally written as it is pronounced. Each vowel has only one sound. The *h* is always silent, and every consonant besides *h* is pronounced when it appears in a word. English, in contrast, has thirty vowel sounds. English consonants are often

More than one hundred thousand people of Chinese ancestry live in Cuba. Some are the descendants of Chinese people who moved to Cuba in the 1800s to work on sugar plantations while many more are from families that migrated from China in the twentieth century.

Cuban women chat on a street in Havana.

silent, such as the *b* in *lamb* and *comb*, the *p* in *pneumonia*, and the *k* in *knuckle* and *knife*.

For foreign speakers, the toughest challenge in Spanish pronunciation is *rr*, the double *r*. It sounds a little like the rumble of a car motor starting up. Try rolling the *r* in the word *perro* (dog). Rest your tongue lightly behind your front teeth and let it vibrate as you say "perro."

In written Spanish, a vowel sometimes has an accent mark to show that it is stressed when the word or name is pronounced. Spanish punctuation is unique because a question

Talk Like a Cuban!

Here are a few Spanish phrases that you are likely to use on a visit to Cuba.

Hola	Hi
¿Cómo está usted?	How are you?
Estoy bien, gracias.	I am fine, thank you.
¿Cómo se llama?	What is your name?
Me llamo...	I am called...
¿Cuántos años tiene?	How old are you?
¿Va llover esta tarde?	Will it rain this afternoon?
No, hace mucho sol.	No, there is plenty of sun.

begins and ends with a question mark, though the question mark at the beginning of the sentence is upside down. Likewise, a sentence that ends with an exclamation point has an upside down exclamation point at the beginning.

A young girl writes in Spanish on a blackboard in a school in Cuba. Everyone in Cuba learns Spanish.

CHAPTER 8

Prayers and Spirits

Each September 8, thousands of Cubans pour into El Cobre, near the city of Santiago de Cuba, to worship at the Basilica of Our Lady of Charity. Our Lady of Charity is the patron saint of Cuba, and her feast day is celebrated throughout the nation. Yet Cubans also honor another female figure, a goddess called Ochún. In Cuba, Roman Catholicism and the African religious practice called Santeria exist comfortably side by side.

Opposite: **A Catholic priest blesses a woman at a church in Rincón, south of Havana.**

The Silence of the Bells

Before Fidel Castro came to power, about 90 percent of all Cubans described themselves as Roman Catholics. The Catholic Church presided over their baptisms, weddings, and funerals. However, only a small percentage of Cubans attended Mass regularly.

CHAPTER 9

Body, Heart, and Mind

EVERY FEBRUARY, CUBANS IN HAVANA FLOCK TO opening events of the International Book Fair. Over the following weeks, the fair spreads across the country, ending in Santiago de Cuba. The book fair is an extravaganza of literary readings, art exhibits, and evening concerts. Everywhere books are on display, a tribute to Cuba's commitment to literacy. Each year the government dedicates the fair to a particular Cuban writer.

Cuba is known for extraordinary achievements in literature, music, and the fine arts. Its athletes have also earned renown throughout the world.

Telling Cuba's Stories

"I saw here cruelty on a scale no human being has ever seen or expects to see," wrote the Spanish friar Bartolomé de Las

Opposite: **Cuba has a strong ballet tradition. Each year hundreds of students receive training at the Pro Danza school in Havana.**

Bartolomé de Las Casas was the first Spanish writer to expose the atrocities the Spaniards committed against the native population of the Americas.

Casas, one of the first Europeans to write about Cuba. For several years, Las Casas owned property near Trinidad, where Taíno slaves worked the land. Eventually he recognized the evils of slavery, and he spent the rest of his life fighting for the rights of the native people of the Americas. His book *History of the Indies* is an unvarnished account of Spanish atrocities in Cuba and throughout the Caribbean region.

Cecilia Valdés, published in 1882, is regarded as the most important Cuban novel of the nineteenth century. In telling the story of Cecilia, a woman of mixed race, the book examines the interactions between people of different classes and races in colonial Cuba. Its author, Cirilo Villaverde (1812–1894), worked to end slavery in Cuba and to win Cuba's independence from Spain. After being imprisoned by the Spanish authorities, he fled to New York and spent the rest of his life in exile.

Nicolás Guillén (1902–1989) is regarded as Cuba's national poet. Born in Camagüey of mulatto parents, he began to publish his poems during the 1920s. Guillén became a communist in the early 1930s. His first collection of poetry, *Motivos de Son*, drew upon his Spanish and African heritage and his experience of racial discrimination. In *Sóngoro Cosongo* and *West Indies Ltd.*, he wrote about the struggle he witnessed among Cuba's poor. His poetry uses words that imitate the sounds and rhythms of Afro-Cuban music.

Alejo Carpentier (1904–1980) grew up in Havana, the son of European parents. His novel *El Reino de Este Mundo* (*The Kingdom of This World*)

The poetry of Nicolás Guillén often confronted social and political issues. Because of this, he became the national poet of Cuba after the revolution.

was inspired by the story of the slave uprising that led to Haiti's independence in 1803. He also wrote a history of Cuban music.

The poetry of Nancy Morejón (1944–) has been translated into ten languages. In 2001, Morejón became the first Afro-

In poetry, Nancy Morejón explores the mix of Spanish and African influences that created the unique Cuban culture.

Cuban woman to win Cuba's National Prize for Literature. She writes about the black experience, about being a woman, and about revolutionary Cuba.

Like Cuban literature, Cuban art mirrors the influences of both Europe and Africa. Artists in the eighteenth and nineteenth centuries created portraits and depictions of nature. During the 1920s, artists of the Vanguardia movement brought modern art to Cuba from France and Spain. Amelia Peláez del Casal (1896–1968) was born in Yaguajay. She studied painting at the National Art Schools in Havana and later in Europe. She is best known for her murals, which use bright colors and strong black lines.

Wifredo Lam (1902–1982) was a painter of mixed European, Afro-Cuban, and Chinese heritage. His godmother was a Santeria priestess, and Santeria practices had a tremendous influence upon his work. In 1923, he went to Madrid, Spain, to study painting, and he remained in Europe until his return to Cuba in 1941. His paintings fused modernist simplicity with Santeria symbols. His most famous work is

Art Is for Everyone

Havana's National Museum of Fine Arts displays Cuban painting and sculpture from the colonial era to the present. Founded in 1913, the museum opened at its present location in Old Havana in 1954. A nearby building houses the Asturian Center, a sister museum that features European artworks and the art of ancient civilizations.

Wifredo Lam poses in front of his painting *The Jungle*.

The Jungle, completed in 1943. It shows four masked figures emerging from a tangle of foliage.

Catching the Beat

In addition to the Santeria religion, the enslaved Africans who came to Cuba brought a rich musical tradition. African music used a variety of drums and other percussion instruments. Today's bongos, congas, and batá drums are the descendants of the many African drums that came to the Western Hemisphere. Cuban musicians also became masters of the guitar, an instrument popular in Spain.

One of Cuba's earliest composers may have been Teodora Ginés (1530–1598), a freed slave who became a musician at the Cathedral of Santiago de Cuba. She is credited with writing the song "Son de la Má Teodora" (The song about Mother Teodora), which is considered the first Cuban song preserved in musical notation.

Manuel Saumell (1818–1870) is sometimes called the father of Cuban Creole music. Born into poverty in Havana, he played the organ at church and began composing music.

Drumming is central to Cuban music.

He wrote a series of contra dances, which use Spanish and Afro-Cuban styles. The Manuel Saumell Conservatory in Havana keeps his memory alive.

Gonzalo Roig (1890–1970) helped found Cuba's National Symphony Orchestra. His opera, based on the novel *Cecilia Valdés*, was first performed in 1932.

Among Cuba's most popular musical forms is the *son*, the ancestor of today's *salsa* dance. Salsa music first became popular among Cubans, Puerto Ricans, and other Latinos living in New York during the 1970s. Salsa is a lively blend of piano, trumpet, trombone, flute, saxophone, and such percussion instruments as bongos, congas, maracas, and cowbells. From New York, salsa spread to the Caribbean, Central and South America, and around the world.

The Queen of Salsa

Cuban singer Celia Cruz (1925–2003) was known as the Queen of Salsa. Born in Havana, she began performing professionally as a teenager. She quickly became known for her soulful voice, spectacular range, and dazzling style. By the early 1950s, Cruz was performing in countries around the world, and following the Cuban Revolution, she decided not to return home. She eventually settled in the United States, where she became one of the leading figures of Latin music. During her long career, Cruz received many honors and awards, including three Grammys, three Latin Grammys, and the National Medal of Arts, the highest honor the U.S. government awards for artistic achievement.

A fast-paced, modern version of salsa is called *timba*. Timba performers such as La Charanga Habanera draw upon musical forms from outside Cuba, including rap from the United States and reggae from Jamaica.

Timba groups such as La Charanga Habanera first came on the scene in the 1980s, creating a complex new type of dance music.

At the Top of Their Game

Baseball reached Cuba in the 1860s, carried by sailors who had attended college in the United States. In 1868, fans of the new game established the Habana Baseball Club. Soon afterward, an American ship visited Havana, and members of the crew competed with the newly formed Cuban team. To the surprise of both teams, the Habana Club won the game. The Cuban players had beaten a team from the United States, where baseball originated.

Baseball became wildly popular in Cuba. The soaring popularity of the new game disturbed leaders in Spain, who were suspicious of anything to do with the United States. Spanish authorities tried to promote a more Spanish sport, bullfighting. The strategy did not succeed. Baseball had come to stay.

The level of play improved in the 1920s, with the arrival of several African American players from the United States. At that time, African Americans were not permitted to play on major league teams in the United States. Cuba was free from

In Cuba, children do not need a field to play baseball. They often play in the street or anywhere else they have a little space.

such discrimination. African American stars such as John Henry Lloyd began to play winter ball on the island.

Today, Cuban baseball stars sometimes defect from Cuba and head to U.S. shores. They are forced to defect because the communist government forbids players from signing major league contracts while they reside in Cuba. The major league clubs offer contracts worth millions of dollars, a fortune unimaginable to most Cuban workers. In 2014, the Boston Red Sox awarded outfielder and Cuban defector Rusney Castillo a contract worth $72.5 million. The Chicago White Sox also gave a huge salary to Cuba-born first baseman José Abreu. He returned the favor by slugging thirty-six home runs in 2014 and winning the Rookie of the Year Award.

José Abreu is considered one of the best hitters in Major League Baseball.

Knockout!

Cuban boxers have long dominated Olympic competition. Over the years they have won sixty-seven medals, including thirty-four gold. One legendary boxer was the heavyweight Teófilo Stevenson. Stevenson won gold medals in 1972, 1976, and 1980. He was hailed as a national hero. He was offered millions of dollars to defect to the United States and fight professionally, but he rejected the offers. "What is a million dollars against eight million Cubans who love me?" he asked. The whole nation mourned in 2012 when Stevenson died of a heart attack at the age of sixty.

In the belief that athleticism fosters a strong society, Cuba's communist government encourages participation in sports. Government officials often state that only rich Cubans played sports and attended games before the revolution. Today, sports are open to everyone. The Cuban people have responded with a passion to the call for athletic excellence.

Students in Cuban schools are taught basketball, volleyball, gymnastics, and track and field. Those who work under expert coaches refine their skills. With intensive training, Cuban athletes perform extraordinarily well.

Every four years, Cuba sends a team to compete at the Olympic Games. For a nation of its size, Cuba has won a stunning number of Olympic medals. In 2012, Cuba sent 111 athletes to the summer Olympic Games. The Cuban team won fourteen medals, including five gold, to rank sixteenth among the participating nations.

Cuba is an island, and most Cubans and visitors to the island enjoy water sports. With its miles of beaches, Cuba is a paradise for swimmers, divers, and surfers. Sport fishers claim that Cuba is the best fishing destination in the Caribbean.

Cuban teenagers swim in the waters off Havana.

The Old Man and the Sea

While fishing off the Cuban coast, the American writer Ernest Hemingway once caught a huge marlin estimated to weigh nearly 1,000 pounds (450 kilograms). By the time he reached port, however, sharks had devoured most of the fish, which was tied to the outside of the boat. Some people believe that Hemingway used this experience as inspiration when he wrote his classic novel *The Old Man and the Sea* (1952). The novel tells the story of an aging Cuban fisherman who has had eighty-four days of bad luck. At last, on his eighty-fifth day, he hooks a giant marlin and struggles to bring it to shore. *The Old Man and the Sea* was cited as one of Hemingway's master works when he won the Nobel Prize for Literature in 1954.

CHAPTER 10

Among Compañeros

AFTER THE REVOLUTION OF 1959, CUBA'S NEW government encouraged citizens to address each other in a new way. The proper form of address became *compañero* or *compañera*, meaning "comrade." The term *compañero* suggests that all Cubans are equals, and fellow comrades working together to forge a better nation for all.

Where the Cubans Live

After the revolution of 1959, the government took over the mansions of Cuba's wealthy residents. In many cases, the owners had fled, often to the United States. Former servants moved into the grand houses, which usually were divided to form several small apartments. Fidel Castro's government also built apartment blocks in rural areas. Today, apartment buildings tower over cane fields and tobacco plantations where the workers once lived in huts with dirt floors.

Most Cubans live in large family groups. It is common for grandparents and even great-grandparents to live with a young couple and their small children. Aunts, uncles, and cousins may also move into the family home. Life at such close quarters can lead to family tensions, but for the most part Cubans are experts at getting along. Privacy is a rare and precious treat.

Before the revolution, people in the villages lived without electricity or running water. Candles and kerosene lamps provided light after nightfall, and water came from a local well or public tap. Castro's government brought electricity and running water to Cuba's rural people. These critical improvements greatly enhanced the quality of life for Cuba's farmworkers.

An extended family in rural Cuba. Today, Cuban families have an average of one or two children.

Cubilete is a popular game played in Cuba by people of all ages. The cubilete set contains five dice. Each die has a combination of symbols on its six sides: the ace, the king, the queen, the jack, los Gallegos (Spaniards), and los Negros (blacks). By rolling dice from the cup, each player tries to get five dice with the same symbol, the ace being the most valuable. Points are awarded based upon the symbols shown on the dice. The first player to reach ten points wins.

In country and city, however, power outages are a fact of life. Public schedules list the hours when electricity will be available, but unscheduled outages can occur at any time. Nevertheless, the government makes every effort to ensure that hotels and restaurants that cater to tourists have power twenty-four hours a day. Cubans joke that the tourist sections of town are ablaze with lights whenever the rest of the city lies in darkness.

Going to School

In 1959, some 22 percent of Cubans between the ages of fifteen and twenty-four were illiterate, and 60 percent of all Cubans were classified as semiliterate. After the revolution, the new government made a major commitment to education that transformed the nation. Today, Cuba boasts a literacy rate of nearly 100 percent, one of the highest in the world. It has what is considered the best education system in Latin America, and its students perform well compared to students from other countries.

Elementary schools in Cuba have no more than twenty-five children per class.

Under Cuban law, all children between the ages of six and sixteen must attend school. The school year lasts from September to July. Classes in the elementary schools may not exceed twenty-five pupils. All schoolchildren wear uniforms. The school curriculum emphasizes hard work, self-discipline, and patriotism.

Following sixth grade, students enter a program of secondary education. After basic secondary education, students may pursue a technical degree or aim for enrollment at a university. Universities in Cuba include the University of Havana, the University of the East, and Central University of Las Villas.

During the massive literacy campaign of the early 1960s, Cubans studied in makeshift schools at night, often by the sputtering light of kerosene lanterns. Today, the tradition of attending night classes continues to flourish. After work, Cubans flock to schools and other public buildings to take courses on history, literature, science, and more. The

Quinceañera

Turning fifteen is a major event in the life of a Cuban girl. In colonial times, a girl's fifteenth birthday marked her transition into adulthood and meant that she had become eligible for marriage. Families hosted magnificent parties for their *quinceañera*, or fifteen-year-old, introducing her to the available suitors in the neighborhood. Today, many families continue to hold big parties for their daughters when they reach the magical age of fifteen. Mother, grandmothers, and aunts cook for days in preparation. The family may save for years to pay for a band, a photographer, and a gorgeous quinceañera dress.

University for All is a school that offers an array of classes broadcast on educational television covering topics that range from architecture to zoology.

Students at the University of Havana, Cuba's oldest university. It was founded in 1728.

Dining In

Since Cuban families have little money to spare, they rarely eat in restaurants. Instead, people gather at one house or another, forming instant parties. Somehow the host family manages to add extra plates at the table, no matter how simple the fare may be.

Cuban cooking makes use of the many delicious fruits and vegetables that grow on the island. Mangoes, pineapples, and plantains are common ingredients. The plantain is a starchy fruit that looks like a large banana. It can be fried in thin slices

A woman sells pineapples, melons, and other fruit from her stand. Fruit is a major part of the Cuban diet.

called *chicharritas*. Thicker slices are called *tostones*. Corn, rice, and beans are staple foods at most meals. Pork and chicken are popular meats. They are often cooked until the meat is falling off the bone. The foods are enhanced with such flavors as cumin, oregano, garlic, and onion.

The most common breakfast in Cuba is a *tostada*. This is buttered bread that is toasted on a grill. People typically wash down their tostadas with *café con leche*, strong coffee mixed with warm milk. Lunch is typically a sandwich filled with meat, cheese, and pickles, or perhaps an empanada, a pastry filled with meat. The typical dinner is meat, rice and beans, plantains, and a salad. Flan is a favorite Cuban dessert. It is a sweet custard topped with a glaze of slightly burnt sugar. Flan originated in France but soon became popular in Spain and Latin America.

Foods such as pork and fried plantains are staples at the Cuban table.

How to Cook Cuban

Here is a recipe for a delicious Cuban appetizer called *frituras de maíz*, or corn fritters. Have an adult help you with the recipe.

Ingredients

1 cup fresh corn kernels

1 egg, well beaten

1 teaspoon ground anise seed

5 tablespoons sugar

Oil for frying

Directions

Mix all of the ingredients. If the mixture is too liquid, add a small amount of flour. Heat oil in a deep-frying pan. Drop the corn mixture into the oil one spoonful at a time. Stir occasionally to be sure the fritters cook evenly. Remove and cool on paper towels.

Getting Around

With their relatively low income, few Cubans can afford to own an automobile. Those who are lucky enough to have cars take very good care of them. Many Cubans are excellent home mechanics, and they can fix anything that needs fixing in order to keep a car on the road. Many of the automobiles on Cuba's streets were built in the 1950s.

Cuba has an extensive system of public transportation within and between its major cities. For decades Havana was famous for its humped trailer-buses, called camel buses, that could carry up to two hundred passengers. After 2008, these buses were phased out and replaced by buses built in China.

Many of the railroad cars and buses used in Cuba are secondhand vehicles from other nations. In the 1990s, the Netherlands donated a fleet of old buses to the city of Havana. Other buses were bought from or donated by Canada, Spain,

Vintage cars are a common sight on the streets of Cuba.

and the former Soviet Union. Spare parts for this assortment of vehicles are hard to come by, and as many as half of the city buses may be out of commission at any given time.

Having Fun

Each summer the people of Santiago de Cuba take to the streets for Carnaval, a festival of music and dance, floats and banners, food, fireworks, and fun. The *carnaval*, or carnival, began in the 1600s to honor the feast day of St. James. Today the religious element has dimmed, and the spirit of fun has

For many Cubans, dancing is a part of everyday life.

National Holidays

Triumph of the Revolution Day	January 1
Victory of the Armed Forces Day	January 2
Good Friday	April or May
Labor Day	May 1
Anniversary of the Revolution	July 25–27
Independence Day	October 10
Christmas Day	December 25

taken over completely. Neighborhood dance groups called *comparsas* depict local legends and aspects of daily life. People of all ages join the lines of conga dancers that weave through the streets. Men and women wearing elaborate masks, giant figures made of papier-mâché, and musicians with drums and rattles follow the floats.

A delightful festival in December is Las Parrandas de Remedios, held in the town of Remedios and in several nearby villages. According to legend, the festival began in 1829 when a priest asked a group of children to beat on sheets of tin to summon the people to Mass. The festival features a series of children's parades with music, dance, and costumes. The grand finale is a contest between two sections of the town to see which can make the most noise.

The Carnaval de Santiago is the biggest of Cuba's street festivals, but it is not the only one. Havana has a huge carnival each July, culminating in a procession along the Malecón, the city's seafront promenade. Other summer festivals take place in Camagüey and Pinar del Río. On these days, people fill the streets, and the joyful sounds of music and laughter waft through the air.

Timeline

People begin occupying Levisa Rock Shelter in eastern Cuba. **ca. 4200 BCE**

Christopher Columbus lands in Cuba during his first voyage from Europe. **1492**

Spaniards establish their first settlement in Cuba. **1511**

The first enslaved Africans arrive in Cuba. **1517**

Slave rebellions break out across Cuba. **1812**

Carlos de Céspedes frees his slaves and triggers the first war for independence from Spain, the Ten Years' War. **1868**

Slavery is abolished in Cuba. **1886**

José Martí helps launch another war for Cuban independence. **1895**

ca. 2500 BCE The Egyptians build the pyramids and the Sphinx in Giza.

ca. 563 BCE The Buddha is born in India.

313 CE The Roman emperor Constantine legalizes Christianity.

610 The Prophet Muhammad begins preaching a new religion called Islam.

1054 The Eastern (Orthodox) and Western (Roman Catholic) Churches break apart.

1095 The Crusades begin.

1215 King John seals the Magna Carta.

1300s The Renaissance begins in Italy.

1347 The plague sweeps through Europe.

1453 Ottoman Turks capture Constantinople, conquering the Byzantine Empire.

1492 Columbus arrives in North America.

1500s Reformers break away from the Catholic Church, and Protestantism is born.

1776 The U.S. Declaration of Independence is signed.

1789 The French Revolution begins.

1865 The American Civil War ends.

1879 The first practical lightbulb is invented.

CUBAN HISTORY

The Spanish-American War begins. **1898**

The United States withdraws from **1902**
most of Cuba; Cuba becomes
an independent nation.

Fulgencio Batista leads the **1933**
Sergeants Revolt, which
overthrows the government.

Batista again seizes power in a coup. **1952**

Fidel Castro leads an unsuccessful **1953**
assault on the Moncada Barracks in
Santiago de Cuba, hoping to overthrow
Batista's government.

Castro's forces drive Batista from **1959**
power; Castro becomes the head of
a new revolutionary government.

With U.S. backing, a band of Cuban **1961**
exiles launches an unsuccessful
invasion at the Bay of Pigs.

Soviet missiles in Cuba threaten to **1962**
cause a war between the United
States and the Soviet Union.

About 125,000 Cubans emigrate to the **1980**
United States as part of the Mariel Boatlift.

The Soviet Union collapses and **1991**
withdraws its support from Cuba,
ushering in a time of hardship called
the Special Period in a Time of Peace.

Fidel Castro resigns; his brother, **2008**
Raúl Castro, becomes president.

President Barack Obama announces **2014**
that the United States is reopening
diplomatic relations with Cuba.

WORLD HISTORY

1914 World War I begins.

1917 The Bolshevik Revolution brings
communism to Russia.

1929 A worldwide economic depression begins.

1939 World War II begins.

1945 World War II ends.

1969 Humans land on the Moon.

1975 The Vietnam War ends.

1989 The Berlin Wall is torn down as
communism crumbles in Eastern Europe.

1991 The Soviet Union breaks into
separate states.

2001 Terrorists attack the World Trade
Center in New York City and the
Pentagon near Washington, D.C.

2004 A tsunami in the Indian Ocean
destroys coastlines in Africa, India,
and Southeast Asia.

2008 The United States elects its first African
American president.

Fast Facts

Official name: Republic of Cuba

Capital: Havana

Official language: Spanish

Camagüey

CUBA

- • Cities of over 200,000 people
- ○ Other cities
- ✪ National capital
- ∴ Archaeological site

0   150 miles

0   150 kilometers

Cuba

National flag

Caribbean coast

Official religion:	None
Year of founding:	1902
National anthem:	"The Hymn of Bayamo"
Type of government:	Communist state
Head of state:	President
Head of government:	President
Area of country:	42,804 square miles (110,862 sq km)
Coastline:	About 2,100 miles (3,400 km)
Neighboring countries:	Cuba is an island in the Caribbean Sea. Its nearest neighbors are the island of Hispaniola (divided between Haiti and the Dominican Republic), the U.S. state of Florida, Mexico, and the Bahamas.
Latitude and longitude of geographic center:	21°30' N, 80°00' W
Highest elevation:	Turquino Peak, 6,476 feet (1,974 m)
Lowest elevation:	Sea level along the coast
Average daily high temperature:	In Havana, 78°F (26°C) in January, 88°F (31°C) in July
Average daily low temperature:	In Havana, 66°F (19°C) in January, 75°F (24°C) in July
Average annual precipitation:	54 inches (137 cm)

José Martí Memorial

Currency

National population (2014 est.): 11,047,251

Population of major cities (2014 est.):

Havana	2,163,824
Santiago de Cuba	555,865
Camagüey	347,562
Holguín	319,102
Santa Clara	250,512
Guantánamo	272,801

Landmarks:
- ▶ *Bellamar Caves*, Matanzas Province
- ▶ *José Martí Memorial*, Havana
- ▶ *National Museum of Fine Arts*, Havana
- ▶ *San Pedro de la Roca del Morro Castle*, Santiago de Cuba
- ▶ *Zapata Swamp National Park*, Matanzas Province

Economy: Cuba's major agricultural products include sugar, tobacco, citrus fruit, coffee, and rice. Sugar, petroleum products, steel, cement, and medicines are all manufactured in the country. Mining products include nickel, cobalt, and sand.

Currency: Cuba uses two forms of currency: the Cuban peso, or CUP, and the Cuban convertible peso, or CUC. About 25 CUPs equal one CUC, and one CUC is worth approximately US$1.

System of weights and measures: Metric system

Literacy rate: 99%

Schoolchildren

Wifredo Lam

Common Spanish words and phrases:

Hola	Hi
Por favor	Please
Gracias	Thank you
¿Cómo está usted?	How are you?
Estoy bien hoy.	I am fine today.
¿Cuánto cuesta?	How much does it cost?
Cuesta cien pesos.	It costs a hundred pesos.
¿A dónde va?	Where are you going?
Voy a mi casa.	I'm going to my house.

Prominent Cubans:

Fidel Castro (1926–)
Revolutionary leader and president

Raúl Castro (1932–)
President

Celia Cruz (1925–2003)
Singer

Nicolás Guillén (1902–1989)
Poet

Wifredo Lam (1902–1982)
Painter

Antonio Maceo (1845–1896)
Leader in Cuba's wars for independence

José Martí (1853–1895)
Poet and leader in Cuba's war for independence

Nancy Morejón (1944–)
Poet

Teófilo Stevenson (1952–2012)
Boxer

To Find Out More

Books

- Ada, Alma Flor. *Under the Royal Palms: A Childhood in Cuba.* New York: Atheneum Children's, 1998.

- Engle, Margarita. *The Poet Slave of Cuba: A Biography of Juan Francisco Manzano.* New York: Macmillan, 2011.

- Garcia, Luis M. *Child of the Revolution: Growing up in Castro's Cuba.* Sydney, Australia: Allen and Unwin, 2007.

- Guillermoprieto, Alma. *Dancing with Cuba.* New York: Vintage, 2005.

- Hayes, Joe. *Dance, Nana, Dance/ Baila, Nana, Baila: Cuban Folktales in English and Spanish.* El Paso, TX: Cinco Puntos, 2010.

Music

- Buena Vista Social Club. *Buena Vista Social Club.* New York: Nonesuch, 1997.

- Cruz, Celia. *Hits Mix.* Miami: Sony Music Latin, 2002.

- *Cuba.* New York: Putumayo World Music, 1999.

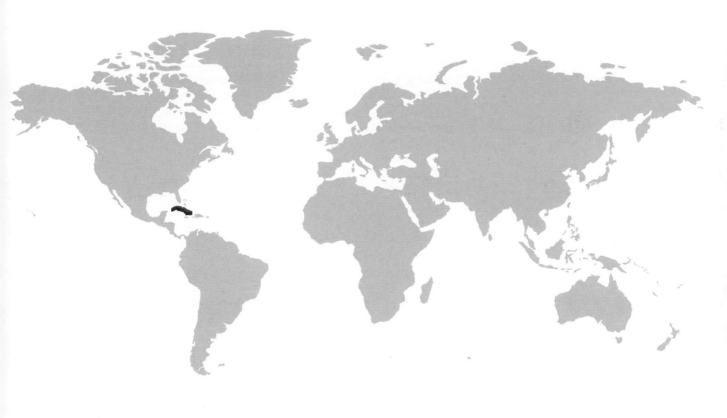

▶ Visit this Scholastic Web site for more information on Cuba:
www.factsfornow.scholastic.com
Enter the keyword **Cuba**

Index

Page numbers in *italics*
indicate illustrations.

A

Abreu, José, 113, *113*
Afro-Cuban people, 40, 43, 87–88,
　　88–89, 89, 106–107, 109
agriculture
　　Alzados (guerrillas) and, 55
　　Camagüey, 20
　　coffee, 45, 46, 82, 83
　　droughts and, 21
　　economy and, 77, 82–83
　　encomienda system, 38–39
　　farmland, 17
　　Fidel Castro and, 53
　　forests and, 25
　　government and, 53, 64, 77, 82
　　harvesttime, *60*, 61
　　hurricanes and, 22, 42
　　literacy rate and, *54*
　　livestock, 31, 82, 100
　　organic methods, 82
　　plantations, 43, 45, *45*, 117
　　slavery, 38–39, 40, 104
　　Special Period in a Time of Peace
　　　　and, 82
　　sugarcane, 45, *45*, 49, 55, *60*, 61,
　　　　82–83, *83*
　　Taíno customs, 91
　　tobacco, 83, 84, *84*
　　United States and, 49, 55
　　War Against the Bandits, 55

Alzados (guerrillas), 55
amphibian life, 25, 31, 33–34, 35
Ancón Beach, 19
animal life
　　Alexander von Humboldt and, 23
　　bats, 29–30
　　birds, 18, *24*, 31–32, *32*, 33, *33*
　　endangered species, 32
　　endemic species, 25, 29, 31, 33
　　horses, 40
　　hutias, 29, *30*, 34
　　livestock, 31, 82, 100
　　mice, 29
　　mongooses, 31, *31*
　　poaching, 32
　　rain forests, 29, *30*, 31, 32, 33
　　rats, 29, 31
　　Santería and, 100
　　Zapata Swamp National Park, 18
Aponte, José Antonio, 43
Arawak people, 37
architecture, 20, *20*, 64, 121
art, 75, 107–108, *108*, 133, *133*
Asturian Center, 75, 108
atheism, 96
automobiles, 61, 79, 125, *125*

B

ballet, *102*
Baracoa, 41, *90*
Baracoa Mountains, 26
baseball, 111–113, *112*, *113*
Basilica of Our Lady of Charity, 95
Batista, Fulgencio, 50, 52, 53
bats, 29–30
Battle of Bayamo, 70
Battle of Dos Ríos, 45
Bayamo, 41, 70
Bay of Pigs invasion, 55–56, *56*
bee hummingbird, 31
Bellamar Caves, 19, *19*
birds, 18, *24*, 31–32, *32*, 33, *33*

Bolívar, Simón, 42
boxing, 114, *114*, 133
"brain drain," 61
Buddhism, 101
butterflies, *33*

C

Cacahual Monument, 89
café con leche (beverage), 123
Camagüey, 20, 87, 105, 127
camel buses, 125
Caribbean Sea, *12*, 13
Carnaval celebration, 126–127
Carpentier, Alejo, 105–106
Carter, Jimmy, 62
Castillo, Rusney, 113
Castle of the Royal Force, 75
Castro, Fidel. *See also* government.
　　agriculture and, 53
　　Bay of Pigs invasion and, 56
　　birth of, 50, 133
　　Che Guevara and, 52, 53
　　childhood of, 50
　　communism and, 52
　　coup of, 51–52
　　Cuban Missile Crisis and, 59
　　Cuban people and, 51, 56, 61, *61*
　　Cuban Steel Company and, 84
　　currency and, 80
　　economy and, 77
　　education of, 50
　　housing and, 117
　　imprisonment of, 51
　　literature and, 107
　　Moncada Barracks assault and, 51
　　presidency of, 52, 53, 55, 56, 57,
　　　　59, 61, *61*, 62, 63
　　religion and, 96
　　resignation of, 63
　　rural development and, 118
　　Soviet Union and, 56, 57, *57*, 59

Special Period in a Time of Peace
and, 78
tourism and, 78
travel restrictions and, 62
26th of July Movement and, 51
United States and, 52, 55
Castro, Raúl. *See also* government.
birth of, 133
Che Guevara and, 52, 53
presidency of, *63*, *63*, 67, 68, 69,
71, 133
Soviet Union and, 56
26th of July Movement and, 51
Catalonian people, 88
Cathedral of Havana, 97, *97*
Cathedral of Santiago de Cuba, 109
Catholic Welfare Bureau, 54
Cauto River, 15, 18
caves, 19, *19*
Cayo Coco, 19
Cayo Guillermo, 19
Cecilia Valdés (Cirilo Villaverde),
104–105, 110
ceiba trees, 27, *27*
Central Intelligence Agency (CIA), 55
Central University of Las Villas, 120
Céspedes, Carlos de, 44, *44*
chicharritas (food), 123
children, 54, 60, *93*, *112*, *116*, 118,
118, 120, *120*, 127
Chinese people, *91*, 101
Christopher (patron saint of Havana),
97
Cienfuegos, 16
cigars, 84, *84*
cities. *See also* Havana; Santiago de
Cuba; towns; villages.
Baracoa, 41, *90*
Bayamo, 41, 70
Camagüey, 20, 87, 105, 127
Cienfuegos, 16
Guantánamo, 87

Holguín, 20, 87
Manzanillo, 16
Matanzas, 16
Sancti Spíritus, 42
Santa Clara, 80, 87
Trinidad, 42
climate, 15, 19, 21–23, *21*, *22*, *23*, 42
clothing, *21*, 61, 65, 120, 121
coastline, *12*, *14*, 15, 16, *16*, 19
coffee, 45, 46, 82, 83, 123
Cold War, 52
Columbus, Christopher, 13, 14, 38,
39, 97
communism, 50, 52, 53, 54, 56, 64,
67, *71*, 74, 96, 105, 114
constitution, 49, 67, 69, 96
Cortés, Hernán, 41
Council of Ministers, 68, *71*, 72
Council of State, 68, 69, 71, *71*, 72
Crimes-Against-the-State Court, 73
Cruz, Celia, 110, *110*, 133
Cruz Varela, María Elena, 107
Cuban Academy of Sciences, 75
Cuban Amazon parrots, 32
Cuban boas, 34, *34*
Cuban convertible peso (currency),
80, *80*
Cuban crocodiles, 18, 34–35, *35*
Cuban emerald hummingbird, *24*
Cuban Missile Crisis, 57–60, *58*, *59*
Cuban peso (currency), 80, *80*
Cuban Revolution, 50–52, *51*
Cuban solenodons, 29, *29*, 31
Cuban Steel Company, 84
Cuban todies, 31, *32*
Cuban tree frogs, 35
Cuban trogon. *See* tocororo.
cubilete (game), 119, *119*
currency
Cuban convertible peso, 80, *80*
Cuban peso, 80, *80*

D
dance, *102*
"Declaration of Cuban Intellectuals"
(María Elena Cruz Varela), 107
Desmarest's hutias, 29, *30*
diseases, 40
Dos Ríos, 10
droughts, 21

E
economy
agriculture, 77, 82–83
business permits, 79
currency (Cuban convertible
peso), 80, *80*
currency (Cuban peso), 80, *80*
employment, 77, 79, *79*, *81*, 85
exports, 81, 85
Fidel Castro and, 77
government and, 64, 77
Great Depression, 50
gross domestic product (GDP),
80–81
imports, 81, 82
manufacturing, 75, 77, 83, 84, *84*
mining, 83, 85, *85*
salaries, 79
service industries, 81, *81*
Soviet Union and, 60, 62, 78
tourism, *49*, 78, *78*, 100, 119
trade, 20, 23, 54–55, 65, 84
education, 54, *54*, 60, 79, *93*, 96, 114,
119–121, *121*
Eisenhower, Dwight D., 55
elections, 50, 68, 69, *69*
electricity, 118, 119
El Nicho Falls, *26*
El Templete building, 27
emigration, 10, 55, *58*, 61–62, *62*, 65,
105, 107, 113, 114
employment, 77, 79, *79*, *81*, 85
encomienda system, 38–39

endangered species, 32, 34–35, *35*
English language, 91–92
executive branch of government, *63*, 67, 68, 72, 73, 133
exiles, 10, 55, *58*, 65, 105, 107
exports, 81, 85

F
families, 118, *118*
Feast of San Lázaro, 97
Figueredo, Perucho, 70
Finlay, Carlos, 49
flan (food), 123
foods, *36*, 76, 77, 79, *79*, 80, 82, 122–123, *122*, *123*, *124*
forests, 25–27, *26*, 28, 31, 32, 33, *36*
Fountain of Love spring, 19
Fountain of Youth spring, 19
frituras de maíz (food), 124, *124*

G
games, 119, *119*
geography
    caves, 19, *19*
    coastline, *12*, *14*, 15, 16, *16*, 19
    elevation, 15, 16
    islands, 14–15, 19
    lakes, 15
    land area, 13, 15
    mogotes (hills), 17, *17*
    mountains, 15, 16–17
    rivers, 15, 18
    waterfalls, *26*
    wetlands, 17–18, *18*, 35
Ginés, Teodora, 109
gold, 38, 41, 42, 85
Gómez, Francisco, 89
Gómez, Juan Gualberto, 49
government. *See also* Castro, Fidel; Castro, Raúl.
    agriculture and, 53, 64, 77, 82
    baseball and, 113

communism, 50, 52, 53, 54, 56, 64, 67, *71*, 74, 96, 105, 114
constitution, 49, 67, 69, 96
Council of Ministers, 68, *71*, 72
Council of State, 68, 69, 71, *71*, 72
Crimes-Against-the-State Court, 73
economy and, 64, 77
education and, 119
elections, 50, 68, 69, *69*
electricity and, 118, 119
employment and, 77
executive branch, *63*, 67, 68, 72, 73, 133
food and, 80
health care and, 80
housing and, 117
independence, 9, *11*, 44, 45, 46, 47, 72, 105, 133
judicial branch, 68, 71, 72–73
laws, 53, 71
legislative branch, 68–69, *68*, 71, 73
manufacturing and, 77
military, *71*, 73
municipal assemblies, 74
National Assembly of People's Power, 68–69, *68*, 71, 72
National Medal of Arts, 110
People's Supreme Court, 68, 71, 72, 73
Platt Amendment, 49
political parties, 67
provincial governments, 72–73, 74
religion and, 96, 100, 101
rural development, 118
"Sergeants Revolt," 50
sports and, 113, 114
State Council, 73
tourism and, 119
Whole Court, 73
Granma (yacht), 51, 53
Great Depression, 50
gross domestic product (GDP), 80–81

Guantánamo, 87
Guantánamo Bay Naval Base, 18, *18*, 48, 49
Guevara, Che, 52, 53, *53*, 80
Guillén, Nicolás, 105, *105*, 133

H
Hatuey (Taíno chieftain), 40, *40*
Havana. *See also* cities.
    Afro-Cubans in, 89
    Asturian Center, 75, 108
    camel buses, 125
    Carnaval celebration, 127
    Castle of the Royal Force, 75
    Cathedral of Havana, 97, *97*
    Christopher (patron saint), 97
    climate of, 15, *22*
    Cuban Academy of Sciences, 75
    Cuban Steel Company, 84
    founding of, 75
    Havana Harbor, 16, 46, 47
    José Martí Memorial, 9, 46, *46*, 75
    Labor Day parade, 66
    La Giraldilla weathervane, 75
    Maine (battleship) in, 46–47
    Manuel Saumell Conservatory, 110
    manufacturing in, 75
    map of, *75*
    Morro Castle, 75
    National Art Schools, 107
    National Library, 9
    National Museum of Fine Arts, 75, 108, *108*
    National Theater, 9
    Old National Capitol, 75, *75*
    old town, 86
    Plaza de la Revolución. *See* Revolution Square.
    population of, 20, 75, 87, 92, *116*
    presidential palace, 52
    Revolution Square, 8, 9, 11, 46, *61*
    roadways in, *22*

Santeria ceremonies in, *100*
Spanish-American War and, 47
Spanish colonization and, 41, *41*
tourism in, *78*
transportation in, 125
University of Havana, 50, 120, *121*
health care, 49, 60, 80, 81, *81*, 85
Hemingway, Ernest, 115, *115*
Hidalgo y Costilla, Miguel, 42
historical maps. *See also* maps.
    Cuban Revolution, *51*
    Early Settlements, *38*
History of the Indies (Bartolomé de Las Casas), 104
Holguín, 20, 87
holidays
    national, 9, 66, 67, 127
    religious, 97, 99
horses, 40
housing, 19, 21, 61, 117
Hu Jintau, 69
Humboldt, Friedrich Wilhelm Heinrich Alexander von, 23, *23*
hummingbirds, 31
hurricanes, 22–23, *23*, 42
hutias (rodents), 29, *30*, 34
"Hymn of Bayamo, The" (national anthem), 70

I

imports, 81, 82
independence, 9, *11*, 44, 45, 46, 47, 72, 105, 133
insect life, *33*, 49
International Book Fair, 103
Isla de la Juventud, *14*, 15, 26, 32, 35, 85

J

James (saint), 126
Jehovah's Witnesses, 101
John Paul II (pope), 96

José Martí Memorial, 9, 46, *46*, 75
judicial branch of government, 68, 71, 72–73
Jungle, The (Wifredo Lam), 108

K

kapok trees. *See* ceiba trees.
Kennedy, John F., 55, 56, 58–59, *58*, 60
Khrushchev, Nikita, 56, *57*, 60
Kingdom of This World, The (Alejo Carpentier), 105–106

L

Labor Day, 66, 67
La Giraldilla weathervane, 75
Lam, Wifredo, 107–108, *108*, 133, *133*
languages, 70, 88, 91–93, *93*
La Patria Libre newspaper, 9–10
Las Casas, Bartolomé de, 39, 103–104, *104*
Las Parrandas de Remedios, 127
Leche Lagoon, 15
legislative branch of government, 68–69, *68*, 71, 73
Levisa Rock Shelter, 37
limestone, *17*, 85
limpieza (Santeria cleansing ceremony), 100
literacy rate, *54*, 103, 119
literature, 103–107, *105*
livestock, 31, 82, 100
Lloyd, John Henry, 113
López, Narciso, 72
Louverture, Toussaint, 43

M

Maceo, Antonio, 89, *89*, 133
Maine (battleship), 46–47
manatees, 30
Manuel Saumell Conservatory, 110
manufacturing, 75, 77, 83, 84, *84*

Manzanillo, 16
maps. *See also* historical maps.
    geopolitical, *10*
    Havana, *75*
    population density, *88*
    provinces, *74*
    resources, *82*
    topographical, *15*
Mariel Boatlift, 62, *62*
marine life, 30, 115
Martí, José, 8, 9–11, *11*, 45, 46, *46*, 75, 133
Matanzas, 16
McKinley, William, 46
measles, 40
Mexico, 41, 42
mice, 29
military, *71*, 73
mining, 83, 85, *85*
mogotes (hills), 17, *17*
Moncada Barracks, 51
mongooses, 31, *31*
Morejón, Nancy, 106–107, *106*, 133
Morgan, Henry, 20
Mormonism, 101
morning glories, 28
Morro Castle, 75
mosquitoes, 49
Motivos de Son (Nicolás Guillén), 105
municipal assemblies, 74
museums, 75, 108, *108*
music, 20, 105, 106, 109–111, *109*, *110*, *111*, 133

N

national anthem, 70
National Art Schools, 107
National Assembly of People's Power, 68–69, *68*, 71, 72
national bird, 33, *33*
national flag, 33, 72, *72*
national flower, 28, *28*

national holidays, 9, 66, 67, 127
National Library, 9
National Medal of Arts, 110
National Museum of Fine Arts, 75, 108, *108*
national name, 14
national poet, 105
National Symphony Orchestra, 110
National Theater, 9
national tree, 26, *26*
New York Journal newspaper, 46
nuclear weapons, 57, 58, 59, *59*

O
Obama, Barack, 65
Ochún (goddess), 95, 99
oil, 81, 85
Old Man and the Sea, The (Ernest Hemingway), 115
Old National Capitol, 75, *75*
Olympic Games, 114
Operation Peter Pan, 54
orchids, 27–28
organic farming, 82
Our Lady of Charity (patron saint), 95, 96, *96*, 99

P
Parque Nacional Alejandro de Humboldt, 23
Peláez del Casal, Amelia, 107
people
    Afro-Cubans, 40, 43, 87–88, 88–89, *89*, 106–107, 109
    ancestors, 90
    Arawak, 37
    Catalonians, 88
    children, 54, 60, 93, *112, 116,* 118, *118,* 120, *120,* 127
    Chinese, *91,* 101
    clothing, *21,* 61, 65, 120, 121
    early settlers, 36, 37

education, 54, *54,* 60, 79, 93, 96, 114, 119–121, *121*
emigration, 10, 55, 58, 61–62, *62,* 65, 105, 107, 113, 114
employment, 77, 79, *79,* 81, 85
encomienda system, 38–39
exiles, 10, 55, 58, 65, 105, 107
families, 118, *118*
foods, *36, 76,* 77, 79, *79,* 80, 82, 122–123, *122, 123, 124*
health care, 49, 60, 80, 81, *81,* 85
housing, 19, 21, 61, 117
languages, 70, 88, 91–93, *93*
literacy rate, *54,* 103, 119
mixed race, 87, 88
pirates, 20, 42, *42*
population, 20, 75, 87, 88
quinceañera parties, 121, *121*
salaries, 79
slavery, 38–39, 40, 43, 44, *44,* 88, 104, 105, 109
Taíno, 14, 37, 38–30, *39,* 40, 90, *90,* 96, 100, 104
travel restrictions, 61–62, 64
voting rights, 69, *69*
whites, 87, 88
women, *92,* 106–107, *106*
Yoruba, 88, 98
People's Supreme Court, 68, 71, 72, 73
Pinar del Río Province, 26, 84, 127
pirates, 20, 42, *42*
plantains, 122–123, *123*
plantations, 43, 45, *45,* 117
plant life
    Alexander von Humboldt and, 23, *23*
    endemic species, 25, 28
    morning glories, 28
    orchids, 27–28
    rain forests, 25–27, *26,* 28
    royal palm tree, 26, *26*

royal poinciana tree, 27
showy chalice vines, 28
white ginger lilies (national flower), 28, *28*
wildflowers, 27–28, *28*
Zapata Swamp National Park, 18, *18*
Platt Amendment, 49
Playa Ancón. *See* Ancón Beach.
Playa de las Coloradas, 51
Plaza de la Revolución, 66
political parties, 67
population, 20, 75, 87, 88
Protestant Church, 101, *101*
provincial governments, 72–73, 74

Q
quinceañera parties, 121, *121*

R
railroads, 49, 52, 125
rain forests, 25–27, *26,* 28, 29, *30,* 31, 32, 33, *36*
rats, 29, 31
recipe, 124, *124*
religion
    atheism, 96
    Basilica of Our Lady of Charity, 95
    Buddhism, 101
    Carnaval celebration, 126
    Cathedral of Havana, 97, *97*
    Christopher (patron saint of Havana), 97
    communism and, 96
    constitution, 96
    education and, 96
    Feast of San Lázaro, 97
    Fidel Castro and, 96
    government and, 96, 100, 101
    holidays, 97, 99
    James (saint), 126
    Jehovah's Witnesses, 101

John Paul II (pope), 96
limpieza (Santeria cleansing ceremony), 100
Mormonism, 101
Ochún (goddess), 95, 99
Our Lady of Charity (patron saint), 95, 96, *96*, 99
Protestant Church, 101, *101*
Roman Catholic Church, 54, *94*, 95–96, 97, *97*, 99
Santeria, 95, 96, 98–100, *98*, *100*
Taíno people and, 40, 100
tourism and, 100
Remedios, 127
reptilian life, 18, 25, 31, 33–35, *34*, *35*
Revolution Square, 8, *9*, *11*, 46, *46*, *61*, 66
Rincón, *94*
roadways, 20, *22*, *23*, 27, 43, 86, *112*, *125*, 127
Roig, Gonzalo, 110
Roman Catholic Church, 54, *94*, 95–96, 97, *97*, 99
Roosevelt, Theodore, 47, *47*
Rough Riders, 47, *47*
royal palm (national tree), 26, *26*
royal poinciana tree, 27

S
salaries, 79
salsa music, 110
Sánchez, Celia, 53, *53*, 133
Sancti Spíritus, 42
San Juan Hill, 47
San Martín, José de, 43
San Pedro de la Roca del Morro Castle, 20, *20*
Santa Clara, 80, 87
Santeria, 95, 96, 98–100, *98*, *100*
Santiago de Cuba. *See also* cities.
  Basilica of Our Lady of Charity, 95
  Carnaval celebration, 126

Cathedral of Santiago de Cuba, 109
climate of, *23*
government in, 42
hurricanes in, *23*
International Book Fair in, 103
Moncada Barracks, 51
population of, 20
port of, 16
San Pedro de la Roca del Morro Castle, 20, *20*
Santísima Trinidad (ship), 75
Saumell, Manuel, 109–110
"Sergeants Revolt," 50
service industries, 81, *81*
showy chalice vines, 28
Sierra Cristal, 26
Sierra de Los Órganos, 16
Sierra de Trinidad, 16
Sierra Maestra, 16, *16*, 51
slavery, 38–39, 40, 43, 44, *44*, 88, 104, 105, 109
smallpox, 40
"Son de la Má Teodora" (Teodora Ginés), 109
Soviet Union, 52, 55, 56, 57, *57*, 58, 59, 60, 62, 78, 126
Spanish-American War, 47, *47*
Spanish colonization
  baseball and, 112
  Battle of Bayamo, 70
  Caribbean conquest, 41
  Christopher Columbus and, 38, *39*
  encomienda system, 38–39
  gold and, 38, 41
  Havana and, 41, *41*
  Hernán Cortés, 41
  José Martí and, 9–10
  Maine (battleship) and, 47
  Mexican conquest, 41, 42
  national flag and, 72
  revolutions against, 42–43

Roman Catholic Church and, 97
San Pedro de la Roca del Morro Castle, 20, *20*
Spanish-American War, 47, *47*
Taíno people and, 38–40
Ten Years' War, 44, 89
"yellow journalism" and, 46, 47
Spanish language, 70, 88, 91, *93*
Special Period in a Time of Peace, 63, 78, 82
sport fishing, 115
sports, 111–115, *112*, *113*, *114*, 133
State Council, 73
Stevenson, Teófilo, 114, *114*, 133
sugarcane, 45, *45*, 49, 55, 60, 61, 82–83, *83*

T
Taíno language, 91
Taíno people, 14, 37, 38–40, *39*, *40*, 90, *90*, 96, 100, 104
television, 121
Ten Years' War, 44, 89
Teurbe Tolón, Emilia, 72
timba music, 111, *111*
tocororo (national bird), 33, *33*
tostada (food), 123
tostones (food), 123
tourism, 49, 78, *78*, 100, 119
towns. *See also* cities; villages.
  Dos Ríos, 10
  Remedios, 127
  Rincón, *94*
trade, 20, 23, 54–55, 65, 84
transportation, 49, 61, 79, 125–126, *125*
Treaty of Paris, 47
Trinidad, 42
Triumph of the Revolution Day, 9
tropical storms, 22
Turquino Peak, 15, 16
26th of July Movement, 51

U

U-2 surveillance planes, 58
United States
　Barack Obama, 65
　baseball and, 112–113
　Bay of Pigs invasion, 55–56, 56
　Central Intelligence Agency
　　(CIA), 55
　communism and, 50, 52, 53, 54
　Cuban Missile Crisis and, 57–60,
　　58, 59
　embassy of, 65
　Fidel Castro and, 52, 55
　Fulgencio Batista and, 50
　Guantánamo Bay Naval Base, 18,
　　18, 48, 49
　José Martí in, 10, 45
　Maine (battleship), 46–47
　Mariel Boatlift and, 62, 62
　military of, 18, 47, 47, 48, 48
　Operation Peter Pan and, 54
　Platt Amendment and, 49
　proximity, of, 13
　railroads and, 49
　relations with, 65, 65
　Spanish-American War, 47, 47
　sugarcane and, 49, 55
　Theodore Roosevelt, 47, 47
　tourism and, 49, 78
　trade embargo, 54–55, 65, 84
　U-2 surveillance planes, 58
　William McKinley, 46
　yellow fever and, 49
University for All, 121
University of Havana, 50, 120, 121
University of the East, 120

V

vaccines, 85
Varadero Beach, 19
villages. *See also* cities; towns.
　electricity in, 118

Fidel Castro and, 118
Las Parrandas de Remedios
　festival, 127
populations of, 87
Taíno, 37, 100
water in, 118
Villaverde, Cirilo, 105
Viñales Valley, 17, 17
voting rights, 69, 69

W

Walsh, Bryan O., 54
War Against the Bandits, 55
War for Independence, 45, 46, 89
West Indies island chain, 14
Weyler, Valeriano, 46
white ginger lilies (national flower),
　28, 28
Whole Court, 73
wildflowers, 27–28, 28
wildlife. *See* amphibian life; animal
　life; insect life; marine life; plant
　life; reptilian life.
women, 92, 106–107, 106

Y

yellow fever, 49
"yellow journalism," 46, 47
Yoruba people, 88, 98

Z

Zapata Swamp, 17–18, 35
Zapata Swamp National Park, 18, 18
zunzuncito. See bee hummingbird.

Meet the Author

DEBORAH KENT GREW UP IN LITTLE FALLS, NEW Jersey. She earned a degree in English from Oberlin College and a master's degree from Smith College School for Social Work and then worked in community mental health in New York City. She had always had an interest in writing and eventually moved to the town of San Miguel de Allende in Mexico to write full-time. Her first young-adult novel, *Belonging*, was published in 1978. Since then, she has written nearly two dozen young adult novels and many nonfiction titles for young readers.

Kent became fascinated with Cuba during high school, when she became friends with a student named Mayra who was among the fourteen thousand Cuban children who came to the United States without their parents through Operation Peter Pan. For four years, Mayra lived with a foster family until her parents were finally able to join her. Until she knew Mayra, according to Kent, Cuba was just another place they talked about on the news. Mayra brought Cuba to life for Kent through her descriptions of the home she had left behind.

Photo Credits